A COMPLETE INTRODUCTION TO

TURTLES

AND TERRAPINS

Terrapene carolina, *the common box turtle.*

Geochelone emys, a tortoise from Southeast Asia. Drawing by Peter Parks.

A COMPLETE INTRODUCTION TO

TURTLES

AND TERRAPINS

Terrapene carolina bauri, *Florida box turtle.*

A COMPLETE INTRODUCTION TO

TURTLES

AND TERRAPINS

Testudo hermanni, *a European tortoise.*

Jo Cobb

SECOND EDITION

© **1987 by T.F.H. Publications, Inc.**

Distributed in the UNITED STATES by T.F.H. Publications, Inc., 211 West Sylvania Avenue, Neptune City, NJ 07753; in CANADA to the Pet Trade by H & L Pet Supplies Inc., 27 Kingston Crescent, Kitchener, Ontario N2B 2T6; Rolf C. Hagen Ltd., 3225 Sartelon Street, Montreal 382 Quebec; in CANADA to the Book Trade by Macmillan of Canada (A Division of Canada Publishing Corporation), 164 Commander Boulevard, Agincourt, Ontario M1S 3C7; in ENGLAND by T.F.H. Publications Limited, 4 Kier Park, Ascot, Berkshire SL5 7DS; in AUSTRALIA AND THE SOUTH PACIFIC by T.F.H. (Australia) Pty. Ltd., Box 149, Brookvale 2100 N.S.W., Australia; in NEW ZEALAND by Ross Haines & Son, Ltd., 18 Monmouth Street, Grey Lynn, Auckland 2 New Zealand; in SINGAPORE AND MALAYSIA by MPH Distributors (S) Pte., Ltd., 601 Sims Drive, #03/07/21, Singapore 1438; in the PHILIPPINES by Bio-Research, 5 Lippay Street, San Lorenzo Village, Makati Rizal; in SOUTH AFRICA by Multipet Pty. Ltd., 30 Turners Avenue, Durban 4001. Published by T.F.H. Publications Inc. Manufactured in the United States of America by T.F.H. Publications, Inc.

Contents

Introduction

It is difficult to imagine why the humble turtle has developed into such a popular pet, especially as it is a reptile — the very mention of which is enough to repulse many people. The four-legged, armored creature we love so much is more closely related to the rattlesnake than it is to a rabbit or hamster, yet we can dote upon it in much the same way as we do with these small, furry animals. Perhaps its superficial resemblance to a small mammal or its slow, ponderous movements make it one of the most loved and venerated of pets.

In spite of their popularity as pets, however, wild turtles of all kinds have not received the treatment they deserve from their human cousins. Commercialization has drastically reduced the wild populations of several species, and this, coupled with the destruction of natural habitats, has brought some kinds dangerously near to extinction.

The author believes that the only way our future generations are going to be able to enjoy chelonian pets is by the institution of properly organized breeding projects *now*. This book is being written with much optimism in the hope that it will help encourage turtle enthusiasts to make every attempt to breed their pets and to obtain pairs for this purpose rather than maintaining just a single specimen.

At the time of writing, a public awareness of the need to conserve *all* endangered species is probably at its highest point ever and, in the not too distant future, it is clear that either complete protective legislation or the total absence of wild stock will preclude the importation of quantities of wild chelonians from their tropical or sub-tropical native habitats into alien temperate lands for use as pets. This could well mean the end of the imported turtle or tortoise as a casual pet, but it will not, and should not, deter the hardened chelonian fanatic. He seeks the pleasure of breeding his charges, just like the budgie breeder or the tropical fish keeper. He wants to be able to supply the demand for pet chelonians without the necessity of further depleting wild populations — although he will never produce enough to restock the wilderness even if the "wilderness" has not been destroyed by pollution and building booms.

It is already encouraging to note that in recent years zoos, private institutions, and some individuals are making progress in the captive breeding of these reptiles, and the *International Zoo Yearbook* has reported several successes with various species. One thing that is going to be increasingly important is the keeping of accurate records and stud books. Any enthusiast should make notes of all types of breeding behavior made by his pets, even if the production of offspring should fail. All happenings should be disseminated by reporting in the journals and newsletters of the various specialist societies. It is only by the systematic coordination of our breeding knowledge of reptiles that any real progress will be made to improve the future prospects of our chelonian friends. This volume is dedicated to that new generation of "cheloniphiles" who will provide their charges with the correct conditions for captive reproduction.

Above: *Today many threatened and endangered species of turtles can be raised in captivity, the young either being released back into nature if the habitat is still suitable or being kept in zoos and parks if the habitat has been destroyed. This young Kemp's ridley,* Lepidochelys kempi, *represents what little hope the species has for a future.*

Evolution, Classification, and Anatomy

Evolution

The first chelonians (a word used to collectively describe tortoises and turtles) appeared on Earth during the mid-Triassic period, some 200 million years ago. One of the first genera of the order Chelonia known to exist was *Proganochelys,* which was similar in many ways to modern tortoises, possessing a high, domed carapace, but differing in having jaws armed with teeth. It is probable that these early armored reptiles developed from small, lizard-like creatures that desperately needed protection from the many carnivorous beasts that abounded at the time. So complete was the protection eventually evolved by the chelonians that they became an extremely efficient group of species that have, almost unchanged, outlived most of their former contemporaries.

The extinct suborder Amphichelydia, which existed from the late Triassic to the Pleistocene periods, contained the family Triassochelidae, of which two genera — *Triassochelys* and *Proganochelys* — are fairly well documented from fossil evidence. The two modern suborders of turtles, Cryptodira and Pleurodira, are direct descendants from the Amphichelydia.

Garden pools like the one shown here attract many other animals besides the ones their owners put into them, and in some areas turtles are among the most common unwanted visitors. Most aquatic turtles will prey on the fishes in the pool and can eat vegetation as well.

Above: *Not eveything with a shell is a turtle! This boxfish,* Ostracion cubicus, *has developed an external shell vaguely similar to that of a turtle, although the ribs are not involved in its shell.*

Classification

Before acquainting oneself with the various living species of chelonians, it is highly desirable to learn a little about the classification of these interesting animals. All animals and plants are scientifically named under a system pioneered by the Swedish botanist Linnaeus in the 18th century. Each animal type is given a name of two parts, the genus and the species, a system called binomial nomenclature. Nomenclature uses mainly Latin as a base, but Greek and other languages may be used in part. A classification of hierarchy relates different groups, each of which contains species with something in common. Species are put in genera, genera are put in families. Families are grouped into orders, and orders with basic similar characteristics form classes. There are five vertebrate (backboned animals) classes: fishes (Pisces), amphibians (Amphibia), reptiles (Reptilia), birds (Aves), and mammals (Mammalia). The vertebrates along with the sea squirts and

Above: *Only about 6000 or fewer species of reptiles still exist today, and they all fall within four main groups. The turtles are a relatively small group of species, but even smaller is the crocodilians, here represented by the alligator,* Alligator mississippiensis.

a few other rather odd marine animals form the phylum Chordata.

Turtles (including tortoises, which are just one family of the entire group) are placed in the class Reptilia. The layman will already know that each species of reptile will have a whole lot in common with all other species of reptiles. Reptiles are unique in having both a scaly skin and highly developed lungs; in fact a reptile could loosely be described as an animal with variable body temperature and possessing both body scales and lungs. These features combine to separate the Reptilia from the other vertebrate classes. Fishes, for instance, also have body scales and a variable body temperature, but no fish has highly developed lungs. Birds may have lungs and also modified scales on their legs, but they maintain a constant body temperature. Mammals have lungs but have hair instead of scales and also maintain a constant body temperature. Thus one has a simple oversight into the classification of vertebrate animals.

In reality this discussion is

of course greatly oversimplified and no class is based solely on such superficial characters. Scientists argue long and loudly on the exact characters and limits — as well as relationships — of all levels from species to phylum.

An explanation of the terms *variable* and *constant* when used in reference to the body temperatures of animals may be appropriate here. Sometimes animals may be described as *cold-blooded* or *warm-blooded,* but these terms are not strictly correct. Fishes, amphibians, and reptiles all have a variable body temperature that can only be regulated by the temperature prevailing in the environment. A certain amount of voluntary temperature regulation can be accomplished by the ectotherms (animals that have a variable body temperature) by behavior, such as moving into or out of direct sunlight. Conversely, endotherms (animals with a constant body temperature) maintain a constant body temperature by internal mechanisms. Man, with his normally constant blood temperature of 37°C (98.6°F) is an example of the latter, while chelonians, being reptiles, are ectotherms.

The class Reptilia is divided into four living orders: Crocodylia (crocodiles, alligators, caimans, and gharials); Squamata (snakes and lizards); Rhynchocephalia (the tuatara, a lizard-like reptile found only on a few islands off the New Zealand coast and sufficiently unique to warrant its own order); and Chelonia (turtles), the order with which we are dealing in this volume. There are of course numerous fossil reptile orders, including the various dinosaurs.

Let's take a well-known species of tortoise and classify it. The Mediterranean tortoise, a popular European species, will do admirably as an example. In the table we will see how this species, resident in so many temperate European gardens, is scientifically classified.

Classification of the Mediterranean Tortoise

Kingdom:	Animalia	All animals
Phylum:	Chordata	Animals with a notochord
Subphylum:	Vertebrata	Vertebrate (backboned) animals
Class:	Reptilia	All reptiles
Order:	Chelonia	All turtles (including tortoises)
Suborder:	Cryptodira	Straight-necked turtles
Family:	Testudinidae	Typical tortoises
Genus:	*Testudo*	Eurasian tortoises
Species:	*graeca*	Mediterranean tortoise

Anatomy

Anatomy

A brief look at the anatomical structure of a typical chelonian perhaps will help us to understand the creatures a little better. Theoretically, the turtle's anatomy is little different from ours; it has all the same parts, but they are put together in a different way! The most obvious part of a turtle is its shell, which most probably arose from a mixture of the rib cage and the original reptilian scaly skin. There are in fact two layers: the dermal shell, which is the well known collection of horny plates, scutes, or laminae that takes the place of normal scales in other reptiles, and the bony plates beneath, which are a fusion of ribs and vertebrae. In chelonians the conventional reptilian scales occur only on the head and limbs and other areas of exposed skin.

The upper part or dome of the shell is known as the *carapace,* while that below is called the *plastron.* The carapace and plastron are joined by bridges that allow for spaces through which the head and limbs can be extended or retracted as necessary. In some species the plastron may be hinged at the front or rear so that the animal can, if it wishes, shut itself away completely from the outside world, as in the typical box turtles. One genus of tortoise, *Kinixys,* even has a hinged carapace that allows

Below: *The turtle's shell is unique among vertebrate structures. Unlike all other vertebrates, the leg girdles (pelvis and shoulders) are actually within the rib cage. The ribs themselves are greatly expanded and fused to form the upper shell, the carapace.*

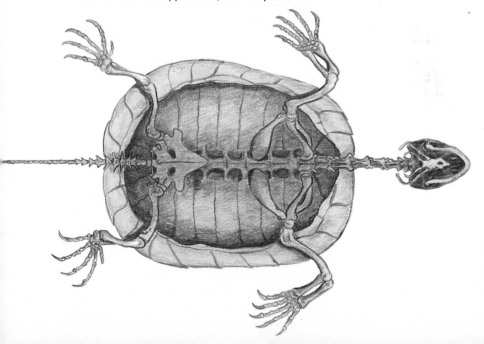

Above: *A pleurodiran turtle, the broad-shelled turtle of southeastern Australia,* Chelodina expansa. *The horizontal position of the withdrawn neck is obvious in this photo.*

added protection for the hind limbs.

The laminae are arranged in a symmetrical pattern on the shell and seldom correspond to the bony plates beneath, thus giving added strength to the shell. Epidermal cells that lie between the two hard layers are the growing part of the shell. As the animal increases in size, new rings of horny material are added to the periphery of each lamina. It is possible to estimate the approximate age of a tortoise by counting these growth rings, but the method is unreliable as the rings tend to wear smooth with time and become indistinguishable; they are also not necessarily in a one-to-one correspondence with age, as they represent growing seasons, not days or months.

Tortoises are unique among the vertebrates in that both the pectoral and pelvic girdles are contained *within* the rib cage, while the main vertebrae are fused to the inner bony plates of the carapace. There are eight vertebrae in the neck of most species, making the head extremely mobile. In the suborder Cryptodira the neck forms a vertical "S" as the head is withdrawn, while in the suborder Pleurodira the "S" is horizontal.

The turtle skull is relatively simple. The bottom jaws are fused at the chin. There are no teeth, but the jaw edges are usually covered with sharp-edged horny plates that perform in the manner of shears.

Turtles and Man

Above: *The red-eared slider or cooter,* Pseudemys scripta elegans, *was well-known to American Indians, was eaten by many people in the South, and was once utilized by the millions for the pet trade. Certainly this turtle has had as much impact on man as has any other reptile.*

Reptiles have captured the imaginations of men since time immemorial, and turtles feature prominently in the folklore of many civilizations. If one delves into the legends and folk stories in various parts of the world it is easy to come up with many examples of the ways in which turtles have affected the lives of so many races of people. It has been the belief of many a primitive race that the earth is supported by a giant turtle. One Indian legend tells of the flat, square earth supported at each corner by an elephant standing on the shell of a giant turtle that is swimming eternally through a sea of milk.

Some North American Indian tribes tell the charming story of the Great Turtle and the Little Turtle. The earth was supported on the back of the Great Turtle but there was no light in the sky. The Great Turtle asked the Little Turtle to ascend into the heavens in order to produce light. So, using a cloud as transportation, she traveled about the sky collecting bolts of lightning that she eventually rolled up into a large bright ball and a small bright ball — respectivley the sun and the moon. The burrowing animals were then asked to make holes in the corners of the sky so that the sun and moon could enter and leave, thus creating the day and the night.

The Hindu god Vishnu takes the form of a tortoise in his second incarnation and becomes Kurma. The ancient Egyptians considered Sheta the Tortoise sacred, and it was a popular subject in various carvings and drawings. The ancient Greeks also showed interest in the chelonians and illustrations of them appear throughout their literature. Statues and toy replicas of the reptiles were also made by both the Greeks and the Romans, and the latter named a certain military formation a "testudo" (a number of men protecting their backs with shields). A Hindu card game features one to ten turtles on each card. The Japanese were and still are very fond of turtles as items of art, and there are many fine pieces of carved ivory and jade depicting the reptiles. In certain areas turtles are said to be endowed with magical healing powers. A native tribe of central New Guinea is convinced that the thigh bone of a river turtle found only in the coastal areas many miles away from their remote villages will remove pain and heal wounds. The tribesmen will pay high prices for such a bone.

Turtles have also provided a source of wholesome meat for many cultures. Sea turtles and their eggs are, of course, well known examples of reptilian cuisine. Happily, the Lord Mayor of London's annual banquet no longer serves the traditional turtle soup. It is less widely known that the Balkan peoples have eaten tortoises for generations — these being the type that are sold as pet animals! Many species of turtles have been and sometimes still are eaten in the Americas, including terrestrial as well as aquatic species. Even the unattractive snapping turtle is classed as a delicacy in some parts of the United States, and there are (true) stories of these reptiles being kept in barrels and fattened up with table scraps until large enough for the pot.

The shells of these animals have also been put to many uses. The well known "tortoiseshell" which comes from sea turtles may be made into masks, combs, or even fish hooks (particularly by the Polynesian peoples), while the same material has become a valuable ornamental commodity in the Western World (though now greatly restricted because of endangered species laws). In Africa and Asia the shells of turtles are used for various things. They may be used as sound boxes for stringed musical instruments, or the women may use them as cosmetic containers. They may even be fashioned into ornamental water flasks.

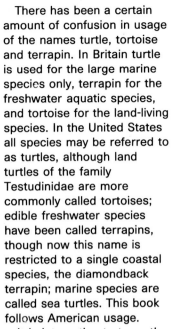

There has been a certain amount of confusion in usage of the names turtle, tortoise and terrapin. In Britain turtle is used for the large marine species only, terrapin for the freshwater aquatic species, and tortoise for the land-living species. In the United States all species may be referred to as turtles, although land turtles of the family Testudinidae are more commonly called tortoises; edible freshwater species have been called terrapins, though now this name is restricted to a single coastal species, the diamondback terrapin; marine species are called sea turtles. This book follows American usage.

It is interesting to trace the origins of the various names. The word *tortoise* probably comes from the Latin *tortus*, which means "twisted," but why it should be so is a mystery. Perhaps it would have been better to use the Latin word for tortoise, *testudo.* The Italians seem to have also developed a word from *tortus* — *tartaruga* — but they also use the word *testuggine.* In Spanish we have *tortuga*, which has obvious connections, as does the French *tortue.* It is from the French *tortue*, which is also derived from the Latin *tortus*, that we get the word

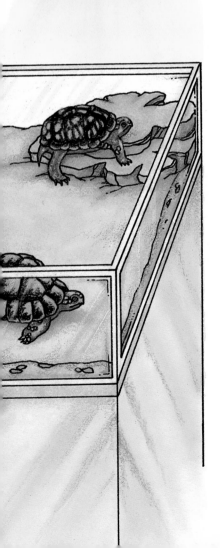

A turtle table is a simple and attractive way to keep a few hardy tortoises or box turtles in the living room.

turtle. It is a good indication of the make-up of the English language that we have derived two different words — tortoise and turtle — from the same source but via different routes. The Germans have their own word, *Schildkrote,* which translated literally means "armored toad." It is not too difficult to understand how this description originated.

Finally, we can hardly terminate this chapter without mention of the Aesops fable that tells the story of "The Tortoise and the Hare". Briefly, the Hare challenges the ponderous Tortoise to a race, knowing that he can hardly lose. So convinced is he that he will win and has plenty of time that he has a nap when halfway around the course. However, he sleeps a trifle too long and the ponderous tortoise gets to the finishing line first. The moral of the story of course is that overconfidence may result in failure.

Below: *In American usage, only the estuarine diamondback terrapin, a close relative of the map turtles, is entitled to the common name terrapin. Once, however, terrapin was applied to any turtle that was commonly sold to be eaten, including especially sliders and cooters.*

Hardy Tortoises

Above: *Two types of Mediterranean tortoises: An old female of the Persian subspecies (larger animal) and a young specimen of the North African form. Both are* Testudo graeca *regardless of details.*

European Tortoises

Hardy tortoises are those that are normally indigenous to temperate or sub-tropical areas and which, given the proper treatment, can live for many years as household pets. These hardy tortoises are the best type for the novice to gain experience with before graduating to the more delicate, exotic varieties. Let us first look at the most familiar hardy European species.

Mediterranean or *Greek Tortoise, Testudo graeca* In spite of its specific name, "*graeca*," this species is not native to Greece but to southwestern Spain and most of northern Africa.

Subspecies are found from Israel, Turkey, and the southern U.S.S.R. to central Iran. The reptile is about 30 cm in total carapace length when adult and has a moderately domed shell. It is easily distinguished from other similar tortoise species of the area by the presence of a bony spur on the rear of each thigh. The shell is a subtle mixture of brown and buff, bordering on the yellowish, younger specimens being noticeably brighter in color. It is fairly simple to distinguish the sexes as the male has a readily recognizable concave plastron, whereas that of the female is quite flat.

In the wild state this

23

species lives in arid semi-desert regions where it subsists on fleshy succulent plants, yellow flowers, and the occasional morsel of carrion. Every year thousands of these reptiles once were exported from northern Africa or Asia Minor to central and northern Europe, where trade was usually very brisk. Imports usually arrived in the spring or early summer, and pet shops 100 to 10,000 at a time. The present legislation in most western European countries has banned the import of these species except under special license.

Statistics showed that over 90% of these unfortunate creatures rarely survived their first year in captivity. The fortunate 10% that were looked after properly, however, made rewarding and

Above: *Hermann's tortoise,* Testudo hermanni, *is more colorful than the average Mediterranean tortoise but it seems to have never become as popular with European tortoise keepers.*

remained well stocked until about early September. After this one rarely saw a tortoise for sale until the following spring. The author has seen tortoises offered by a single wholesaler in quantities of entertaining pets, and there are authentic reports of some specimens reaching over 100 years of age. Further research into their breeding habits is going to be necessary before captive stocks can be maintained, and this is going to be a necessity if wild populations are to be saved. Collecting on such a massive scale for just a few years can only lead to extinction at worst or extreme scarcity at best.

Tortoise keeping is a responsible hobby and one that is not to be taken lightly. The breeding of these reptiles is also a technical matter, and it is only the extremely dedicated and vigilant person with an understanding for the creatures who is ever likely to succeed. In fact, tortoise breeding is such an unusual occurrence in Britain, for example, that success is normally reported in the national press.

Hermann's Tortoise,
Testudo hermanni This was another popular species although imports of these were not quite in as vast numbers as *T. graeca*. It is very similar to *T. graeca* but is usually smaller, being about 25 cm long, and lacks the spurs on the thighs but has a single sharp spine on the tip of its tail instead. The habits of both *T. graeca* and *T. hermanni* are similar, and it seems possible that hybrids occur in the wild where their respective territories overlap. Hermann's tortoise ranges

Below: *Since Hermann's tortoise occurs in Europe proper, it has been imported occasionally into the United States. Like other European tortoises, however, it is very delicate and seldom does well unless given specialized care.*

Above: *The margined tortoise,* Testudo marginata, *is the least common of the European tortoises and the one most rarely kept in captivity.*

from the Balkan Peninsula to Italy and the Iberian Peninsula.

Margined Tortoise, *Testudo marginata* A much scarcer form that occasionally turns up among groups of the other species is the margined tortoise, which is recognized by its larger size, its elongated carapace, and in male specimens by the flared marginal plates at the rear of the shell that give it its name. It is the typical tortoise of Greece.

The three species just described may all be treated similarly in captivity. During the summer months they can be quite safely left outside, providing the temperature does not drop below 16°C (60°F). Even lower temperatures can be tolerated for short periods, but the reptiles will become extremely sluggish and will stop feeding. They are really happy at temperatures of 22°C (72°F) or more, when they will be more active and will feed readily.

Feeding
Once settled into a good routine captive existence, the

hardy tortoise will be found to be fairly cosmopolitan in its diet, so a wide variety of food items should be offered. The basic diet will be greens, much of which they will forage for themselves if allowed to run on a grassy or weedy area. They seem to be particularly attracted to yellow flowers, and a "non-feeder" can often be tempted to become a "feeder" by offering it dandelion flowers. Other favorite "appetizers" are strawberries, gooseberries, and other soft fruits. If fresh fruit is not available then use canned — tortoises are not that fussy!

In addition to allowing your tortoise to eat weeds and grass, he should be given a daily saucerful of varied

Below: *Although the tendency of most beginning tortoise keepers is to feed their charge lettuce, this is actually a poor choice of foods. It is not rich in nutrients and may also cause diarrhea.*

foodstuffs. A combination of two or more of the items suggested in the table can be given, and it is wise to add a sprinkling of a multivitamin and/or a calcium compound over each meal to help keep your pet in the best of health. A little cod-liver oil occasionally is also beneficial.

Contrary to popular belief, tortoises are not notorious destroyers of insect pests, and slugs or snails have little to fear when the tortoise is on the rampage. However, they are not averse to devouring the odd bit of carrion if it comes their way, and this little extra could be important in maintaining the animal's health. In captivity the carrion can be replaced by a few pieces of minced meat two or three times a week. Some tortoises will even take canned dog or cat food or even steak and kidney pie. All food offered to your tortoise should preferably be chopped into bite-sized pieces, for, unlike in the wild, there is an absence of the helpful leverage supplied by the living food plant as the reptile tears a piece off.

List of foods suitable for most species of tortoise
Appetizers
(to be given when other foods fail to interest)
Strawberries
Gooseberries
Peaches
Apricots
Young green peas
Runner beans
Rose petals
Dandelion flowers
Buttercups
Rose hip syrup (sprinkled over food)
Clover

Staple Diet
(to be given daily and varied)
Shredded cabbage
Shredded lettuce
Grated carrot
Sliced apple
Sliced pear
Sliced banana (including skin)
Sliced tomato
Brown bread
Cereals (with milk or without)
Clover
Grass
Dandelions
Plantains
Minced lean meat
Canned cat food
Canned dog food

Supplements
Cod-liver oil, calcium orthophosphate, various vitamin/mineral preparations

Hibernation
There are differing schools of thought on the hibernation of tortoises. It is, of course, only the species that live in temperate climates that actually hibernate; tropical tortoises either have no rest period at all or there is a period of estivation.

With regard to the European tortoises, some authors advocate artificial hibernation, but others maintain that the animals should be kept warm and active during the winter months. I have found that, without doubt, more reptiles are lost in hibernation than if they are not allowed to hibernate.

Based on an average number of 15 to 20 tortoises during the period 1971-78, the following statistics are of interest. During the winters of 1971, 1972 and 1973, the tortoises were hibernated in straw-packed boxes in a cold outhouse in the manner prescribed in most tortoise literature. An average of 25% of the total was lost in each of the winters and in the critical period of recovering from the hibernation. In the winters of the following four years all the tortoises were kept just awake at a temperature of 12°C (54°F) in a heated tortoise house. The reptiles also had the added opportunity of being able to further increase their temperature by basking under an infra-red heat lamp. Strangely, the tortoises did not want to spend all of their time under the heat lamp and most took prolonged periods of rest under the piles of straw that were available in the house. Most of them fed once or twice per week during the winter period but, it is stressed, they were given the opportunity to do what they wished — there was no period of forced hibernation. Treating the animals in this manner, there were no deaths directly attributable to the winter "hibernation" period, although about 5% were lost

Below: *A very small percentage of Mediterranean tortoises do live to a ripe old age in captivity, either because their owner has a certain knack for keeping them or because they are somehow better suited to adjust to captivity than their cousins.*

through other causes.

It is suggested that the reasons for this are that the latter treatment for the animals provides conditions not unlike those of their native habitats. In Europe most of the imported tortoises come from either northern Africa or Turkey, where, according to the distribution maps, the majority occur along the coastal strips. If one studies temperature charts of these areas it will be found that the winter temperatures are rarely excessively cold for long periods and on many days it is quite warm enough for a tortoise to be able to be out and about. Therefore it is most unlikely that the dormant period for wild tortoises is anywhere nearly as long as the period for which they are expected to hibernate in northern Europe.

Another aspect that is important is the excessive dampness that is common to northern winters. Indeed, many tortoise deaths during hibernation can be related to coldness *and* dampness

Below: *Horsfield's tortoise, also called the Afghan tortoise, is a small species that is quite cold-hardy. The rounded carapace and the presence of only four claws on the front feet make it quite distinctive. When available (which is rarely) it makes a fairly good pet. Its natural habitat is the dry, frigid steppes of western Asia.*

Above: *The common gopher tortoise of the southeastern United States was once a fairly common pet, but it is now listed as threatened in several states. It rarely does well in captivity anyway, so it is best to pass it by if you should see it offered.*

rather than just coldness.

It is therefore advocated that when sub-tropical chelonians are removed from their habitat and transported to higher latitudes, an attempt should be made to simulate as near as possible the animal's original environment.

American Tortoises

Hardy species of tortoise that at one time occurred on the American market and may have occasionally arrived in Europe are now to be considered. Enthusiasts in the United States were once fortunate in being able to collect some of their own specimens from the wild, but now in most states tortoises are protected and collection forbidden or limited. The prospective collector should therefore ensure he is aware of state regulations before taking any tortoises.

Gopher Tortoise, *Gopherus polyphemus* This is the typical North American tortoise and was once fairly abundant in the southeastern states, including the Carolinas, Georgia, Alabama, Mississippi, and Florida. An adult specimen averages 25 cm in length and individuals of 35 cm occasionally occur. The basic shell color is dark brown to black with a blotchy pattern of lighter browns. The head and limbs are shiny black. The forelimbs are flattened into a shovel shape, an adaptation for burrowing into sandy areas. Gopher tortoise burrows may be anything up to 12 m in length, and the sleeping chamber at the end can be up to 3 m below the surface. The burrows of gopher tortoises

In some country districts gopher tortoises are still used by the people as food items and are dragged from their burrows by hooks on the end of long flexible poles. The flesh of the gopher tortoise is called "low ham." Such practices are now largely forbidden because of

Above: *The Bolson tortoise of Mexico,* Gopherus flavomarginatus, *is the largest American gopher tortoise. Amazingly, it was only discovered by scientists in 1959. Specimens are kept in many zoos, but few individuals have it.*

are often used as retreats by other animals such as rats, rabbits, raccoons, gophers, opossums, indigo snakes, and lizards. Even rattlesnakes are said to live peacefully with the other inhabitants when they are at home.

declining numbers of gopher tortoises.

These reptiles are largely herbivorous, and captive specimens should be fed a variety of fruits and vegetables. In the wild they are nocturnal and spend most

Above: *Although it was once widely adovcated as a wonderful pet, the desert tortoise,* Gopherus agassizi, *is actually very hard to maintain in captivity unless you can give it special care and have a magic touch. In fact, its very collection is outlawed in most of the states where it occurs in the southwestern United States and some states have even outlawed possession of a specimen.*

of the daylight hours in their burrows. In captivity they may become semi-diurnal but should be provided with a sandy area in which they can burrow. Because they are often delicate and no longer abundant, most American herpetologists now recommend that gopher tortoises (and all *Gopherus* species for that matter) not be kept as pets.

Texas Tortoise, *Gopherus berlandieri* Only about half the size of the preceding species, the Texas tortoise is found in the southern parts of Texas and in northeastern Mexico. It is less hardy than the gopher tortoise and would

require extra heat during the winter months. Not suitable as a pet.

Desert Tortoise, *Gopherus agassizi* This is a larger species from the American Southwest reaching about 30 cm in length. It is difficult to keep in colder climates unless it is housed in a desert vivarium. Various types of cacti and other desert plants are the wild desert tortoise's staple diet, and from these they are able to extract large quantities of water that they store in their specialized bladders for quite long periods. They will not survive for long in damp conditions and are not suitable as pets.

Tropical Tortoises

In this chapter it is intended to deal with those tortoises that if kept in captivity in a temperate climate will require heated indoor accommodations. While there may be some argument on the subject of hibernation in the Mediterranean species, it is definite that the tropical species should be kept warm throughout the year. Most of the exotic tortoises that are frequently imported are at first delicate and difficult to acclimate to their artificial environment. Nearly all of the savannah and semi-desert species will, most definitely, be unable to cope with humid conditions, so housing is of prime importance when keeping these species. Once a tropical species gets over the shock of being captured and transported to a completely different climate, acclimates itself to its new accommodations, and begins to take in a healthy quota of nourishment, it will settle down and give its owner years of pleasure.

AFRICA

Spurred Tortoise, Geochelone sulcata
This species is probably the largest of the African mainland tortoises, a specimen weighing in excess of 85 kg and 75 cm in length having been recorded. It is named after the two hard spurs that are found on the rear of each thigh. It is a rather plain yellow color all over, and there are deep serrations between the anterior marginal plates. Being mainly herbivorous, it subsists on the fleshy and sparse vegetation of its semi-desert habitat but will occasionally take carrion if available. In captivity it will take most items mentioned for the hardy tortoises, including the occasional piece of meat. It is found in the southern part of northern Africa, ranging from Eritrea in the east to Senegal in the west.

Leopard Tortoise, Geochelone pardalis
This very attractive tortoise is extremely popular as a pet but is only occasionally available. The main carapace color is yellow with black blotches, hence the word "leopard." It is found from southwestern Africa to the Sudan in the north and down to Natal. The maximum size is 50 cm in length and a weight of 30 kg. It is very fond of fruit but will take most of the usual tortoise foods.

Radiated Tortoise, Geochelone radiata
This attractive species and the closely related G. yniphora are confined to the island of Madagascar. The former has starred markings similar to the familiar starred tortoise but grows much larger (45 cm), while the latter has a plain sandy coloration. The famous Tui Malila, a tortoise reputedly presented to the

Above: *The leopard tortoise*, Geochelone pardalis.

Below: *A hatchling radiated tortoise*, Geochelone radiata.

Queen of Tonga by Captain Cook in 1777 and which died in 1966, was found to be a radiated tortoise.

Pancake Tortoise, *Malacochersus tornieri*

Mentioned here because of its popularity as a bizarre pet, the pancake tortoise is unusual in having a very flat appearance almost as though it had been run over by a steam roller. The shell is soft and the animal protects itself by lodging into rock crevices and inflating its lungs, thus rendering itself almost immovable to any predator. It will take the usual tortoise foods in captivity and soon becomes a friendly and

35

Tropical Tortoises

Above: *The very un-tortoise-like pancake tortoise,* Malacochersus tornieri. *Its flattened and very flexible shell allows it to move very fast for a turtle and even wedge itself into cracks between rocks.*

intelligent terrarium inmate. In the author's experience this species has been suspected of biting pieces off various lizards that shared its accommodations.

Hinge-backed Tortoises, *Kinixys* Another genus of bizarre tortoises is the hinge-backs, of which there are three closely related species. They have a hinge of cartilaginous material toward the rear of the carapace that has been developed to protect the rear end of the animal from predators. The most well-known species is

Bell's hinge-back, *Kinixys belliana,* which grows to about 25 cm in length. It prefers savannah country in a wide area of tropical Africa. The forest hinge-back, *Kinixys erosa,* is somewhat larger and prefers thickly wooded regions in the same area, while the third species, *Kinixys homeana,* is much smaller, rarely exceeding 20 cm.

Geometric Tortoises, *Psammobates* These are tortoises with a starred or radiating pattern on the shell and a body seldom more than

Above: *In* Kinixys belliana, *one of the hinge-backed tortoises, the back part of the upper shell is actually hinged, allowing the tortoise to close the rear end of the shell.*

Below: *The small parrot-beaked tortoise,* Homopus areolatus, *makes a fairly good pet if you can find a specimen.*

12 cm in length. The three closely related species are *Psammobates geometricus*, *Psammobates tentorius*, and *Psammobates oculifer*, all found in parts of South Africa and surrounding areas.

Parrot-beaked Tortoise, *Homopus areolatus*

There are four South African species in the genus *Homopus*, the best known of which is the parrot-beaked tortoise, a very small animal fully grown at 11 cm. The other species are *H. boulengeri*, *H. signatus*, and *H. femoralis*.

Below: *The distinctive hourglass shape or pinched waist of the carapace of the red-legged tortoise,* Geochelone carbonaria, *is one feature that separates it from the similar yellow-legged tortoise.*

SOUTH AMERICA

There are three *Geochelone* species found on the mainland of South America:

Yellow-legged or Jaboty Tortoise, *Geochelone denticulata*

The yellow-legged tortoise (sometimes known as the jaboty, Hercules, or Brazilian giant tortoise) is a shy forest species which spends most of its time lurking in thick undergrowth in northern South America, where it feeds on leaves, fruits, and the occasional insect. It has an elongated carapace, mainly dark brown with a yellowish blotch in the center of each lamina, while some of the scales on the head and limbs are yellowish orange in color. The average length is 35 cm, although there are records of specimens twice this length.

In captivity it is very fond of fruit and will take meat. Wild specimens are said to be especially fond of plums, and the presence of half-eaten wild plums is an indication that the tortoises are in the area. It is used extensively by the Amerindians as a food item.

Red-legged Tortoise, *Geochelone carbonaria*

Closely related to the preceding species but with a much wider range from Panama to Paraguay, the red-legged tortoise has a darker shell (usually black) with lighter markings on the laminae. This animal gets its

Above: *A beautifully colored, healthy specimen of the red-legged tortoise. If given proper care and a varied, nutritious diet this species makes a fine pet.*

name from the prominent scarlet scales on its front limbs. It is more cosmopolitan in its habitat than *G. denticulata* and may be found on open savannah or in deep forest in various parts of its range. Its average length is 27.5 cm, but it reaches at least 40 cm.

Argentine Tortoise, Geochelone chilensis This is the third South American tortoise, and it is much smaller than the other two, seldom exceeding 20 cm in body length (but reaching over 40 cm). It is found in the more arid regions of central South America, where it relies on its somber yellowish coloration for camouflage. This may be a complex of three species.

ASIA

Burmese Brown Tortoise, Geochelone emys One of the larger Asian tortoises, *G. emys* may grow up to 60 cm in length. It has a large head and limbs and is predominantly brown in color. It is found in the hilly regions of Burma, Thailand, and Malaysia.

Above: *The seldom imported Argentine tortoise,* Geochelone chilensis. *The scientific name is misleading, as the species probably does not occur in Chile.*

Below: *Also seldom imported is the large Burmese brown tortoise,* Geochelone emys.

Above: *Perhaps the most attractive tortoise is the Indian starred tortoise,* Geochelone elegans. *Once common on the pet market, its import is now heavily involved with red tape and it is not commonly seen. It is also very subject to pneumonia.*

A smaller, closely related species, *Geochelone impressa,* is found in the same area, and a third species, *G. forsteni,* which is smaller still, is found on the Celebes (Sulawesi) Islands.

Elongated Tortoise, *Geochelone elongata*
This species is found from northern India through Burma and Thailand to central Malaya. It grows to about 30 cm in length and, as its name implies, its carapace has an elongated appearance. A closely related species, *G. travancorica,* is found further south in peninsular India.

Starred Tortoise, *Geochelone elegans*
One of the most frequently imported species of exotic land tortoises was the starred tortoise of India and Sri Lanka. The carapace laminae

are slightly conical and a black "star" pattern on yellow radiates from the center of each one, giving an extremely pleasing effect. It is another predominantly fruit-eating species, but it will also take green food and a little meat. The maximum size is about 25 cm. Because of restrictive export legislation in India, the species is not commonly seen today in pet shops.

Another closely related "starred" tortoise is *Geochelone platynota* from Burma, which is very similar to the preceding species but a little smaller and with more yellow on the carapace.

Giant Tortoises

While it is highly unlikely that many private individuals will ever keep giant tortoises in captivity, one can hardly

publish a book on turtles without a mention of these magnificent beasts. Also, it is a distinct possibility that some of the subspecies may only be saved by captive breeding programs.

Galapagos Giant Tortoise, *Geochelone elephantophus* The Galapagos Islands, which lie 660 miles west of Ecuador in the Pacific Ocean, have been the subject of much discussion ever since Charles Darwin wrote about his sojourn there in his *Voyage of the Beagle* in 1835. Many of the animals that occurred on the islands were studied by Darwin, and the differences and similarities of animals on the various islands formed part of the basis of his theory of evolution.

The giant tortoises of the Galapagos were no exception to this rule and each island was found to possess its own subspecies especially adapted to life on that island. There are still about 10 subspecies of these tortoises in existence, but several subspecies have become extinct since their discovery (and most probably because of it). There are two major groups of Galapagos tortoises, the "saddleback" type and the "domeshell" type. The saddlebacks live on arid islands where food has to be reached high in the vegetation, while the domeshells live in damper areas where food may be grazed directly from the ground. Most of the subspecies are plain grayish in color. They may range in size from 90 cm and 40 kg to 120 cm and up to 570 kg.

Left: *Galapagos giant tortoises,* Geochelone elephantopus, *are commonly seen in zoos and parks.*

Above: *Another favorite of zoos and parks is the Aldabra giant tortoise,* Geochelone gigantea. *This large species exists in incredible numbers on its very small and seemingly very barren home islands.*

Aldabra Giant Tortoises, ***Geochelone gigantea*** The sole surviving species of Indian Ocean giant tortoises is the Aldabra, *Geochelone gigantea,* which due to protection and isolation still abounds on its small island home in gigantic numbers. It is the species of giant tortoise most frequently seen in zoos. On its native island it feeds mainly on the sparse available vegetation but will take carrion when available. It has been known to consume the bodies of animals washed up on the shore, including whales!

In captivity this species will eat almost anything offered to it, and in zoos it has been known to take ice cream, ham sandwiches, and cheese crackers from the public! Their rate of growth is amazing — it may take only 4 years for a 5-cm hatchling to reach 50 cm in length.

Emydid Turtles

In this chapter we will deal with some of the species belonging to the family Emydidae — typical American and Eurasian aquatic turtles — most commonly offered by dealers. In most cases these species are pretty hardy and adaptable to captive conditions. A word of warning however: the very small hatchlings sometimes available are not easy to rear and require a great deal of attention for the first two or three months. Once settled into captive life, however, and given the correct requirements, the reptiles become extremely hardy and can give their owner much pleasure. In the United States,

Below: *The distinctive head markings and general appearance identify this turtle as a slider or cooter,* Pseudemys, *but the actual species is very hard to determine. The long claws on the front feet mark this as a male.*

sales of most turtles under 4 inches (10 cm) in carapace length are prohibited because of possible *Salmonella* contamination (food poisoning bacteria), but they may still be collected and are exported in large numbers to Europe.

The species most widely available in Europe (and formerly in North America) is the red-eared slider (from its habit of sliding into the water off basking logs), *Pseudemys scripta elegans.* Thousands of hatchlings of this species are exported from the southern United States to Europe, and formerly hundreds of thousands were sold in the United States. The young reptiles are only some 3-4 cm in length and are usually a mixture of dark green and yellow colors. At this stage they are often difficult to acclimate to captivity and may refuse to feed; countless numbers of the little creatures perish because they are purchased by persons ignorant of their requirements.

Whatever the species to be kept, young emydid turtles mostly have similar basic requirements to enable them to grow up into healthy adults. They must be supplied with a certain amount of light and heat, natural sunlight being the best but supplemented by an artificial source should the former be in short supply. Before purchasing young turtles a suitable terrarium should be prepared. For a trio

of young red-ears a tank 60 cm x 35 cm x 35 cm deep would be ample. The type of tank is of little importance, but the advent of silicone sealers has made the all-glass tank cheaper than older metal-framed tanks. As the water will require frequent changing, little furnishing will be required, although two rocks — one at each end of the tank — placed so that they just break the surface of the water will ensure that the turtles do not drown (which they will if unable to land). About 15 cm over one of the rocks a 40-watt light bulb is hung so that the little reptiles can "sunbathe." The rock at the other end of the tank will ensure that they also have a cooler landing point. An additional broad-spectrum fluorescent light fitted into the tank hood would be extremely beneficial but should be used not more than four hours per day, as too much ultra-violet light can be as damaging as too little.

The temperature of the water should not be allowed to drop below 18°C (65°F) at night and may be allowed to go as high as 30°C (86°F) during the day. The gradual changes in temperature between night and day are beneficial to the reptiles, but sudden changes such as may occur when the tank is cleaned must be avoided. Whenever fresh water is added to a tank, the turtles should be first removed into a dry container and the

Above: *Once literally millions of baby red-ears,* Pseudemys scripta elegans, *were bred and collected for the pet market. Since the growing fears of salmonellosis (food poisoning) being transmitted from turtle to man led to size restrictions on salable turtles, baby red-ears have disappeared from the American market. They are still popular in Europe and Japan, however.*

Below: *The Big Bend slider of Texas,* Pseudemys scripta gaigeae. *Note the two red spots on the head.*

temperature should be brought back to the previous temperature by the addition of warm water before returning the reptiles. Thus a thermometer is an important item in a terrapin keeper's equipment. The water itself can be heated using an ordinary aquarium heater and a thermostat. The enthusiast may even contemplate having a system of time switches, dimmers, and thermostats so that a natural "dusk to dawn" effect can be simulated. It is possible, with a little imagination and a little help

Homopus areolatus, *a South African parrot-beaked tortoise.*

from an electrician, to simulate a climate almost identical to that of the animal's natural habitat, and the further addition of "seasons" could well encourage the creatures to breed more readily in captivity. It is a good idea to find out where the particular species comes from and then to consult an atlas in order to ascertain the animal's climatic requirements.

Most turtles are mainly carnivorous in the wild and feed largely upon insects, molluscs, crustaceans, fishes, and amphibians. They are partial to carrion, and a few emydid turtles will soon reduce a dead rodent to a skeleton. Some species take larger amounts of green food, especially when adult.

Most of the many species of aquatic turtles the author has kept have thrived on a predominantly carnivorous diet, but many will take the odd bit of shredded lettuce or even small pieces of apple or banana. With very young turtles, red-ears for instance, the following menu is recommended for each animal per day:

1-2 grams minced lean beef or chopped earthworm or tubifex, plus a very small quantity of chopped lettuce or apple or other fruit, plus a vitamin/mineral supplement. As the reptiles grow the amounts of food are gradually increased. Turtles (and tortoises) are very susceptible to a condition known as "soft shell" should they receive a diet deficient in certain vitamins and calcium. To combat this a multivitamin supplement plus a calcium-based supplement can be worked into the meat before each meal. It is a good idea to ask your veterinarian to recommend the best type of supplements available in pet shops in your area. As soon as your young terrapins are used to feeding in captivity it is advisable to remove them to a smaller container at mealtimes. This will ensure greater hygiene in their living quarters as the water will not become as polluted with uneaten food. In any case, hygiene is very important in the keeping of aquatic turtles, and fouled water should be changed frequently — but not forgetting to bring the temperature back up to its previous level before reintroducing the inmates.

The emydid turtles *must* be allowed to bask in the sun or a light to clean the shell and produce vitamins necessary for good, hard shells. Provisions for basking must be available to all aquatic emydids at all times, whether you are keeping hatchlings or adults.

As your turtles grow they will require a larger tank, or if breeding is to be contemplated, a specially built vivarium. In some areas it is possible to keep turtles in a outdoor pool for at least part of the year (although they may have a tendency to wander

Above and below: *These small hatchlings of* Pseudemys scripta *will need a large tank, plenty of nutritious food, and suitable lighting and temperatures before they will grow up. Soft shells are a major problem in raising baby sliders, but this can be prevented by using vitamins and calcium blocks.*

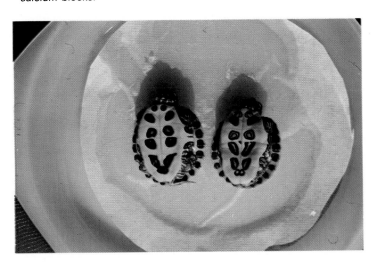

away occasionally).

Turtles of 10 cm or more in length will also be looking for a more varied diet, and any of the following can be given in varying quantities:

Lean meat, offal, dead whole or chopped up day-old chicks, dead mice, canned dog or cat food, trout pellets, whole sprats or strips of herring, boiled eggs, mealworms, maggots, or locusts and any other insects

51

Above: *Typical red-ears,* Pseudemys scripta elegans. *The irregular scutes of the larger specimen are fairly common in specimens raised in captivity. A red-ear is most subject to diseases and deficiencies during its first year or so of life, when it is actively growing. Unless provided with an adequate diet and all the minerals it needs for shell growth, it will not survive more than a few months.*

that can be caught, earthworms, snails, the occasional scrap of green food, and (often greatly favored) a little banana. Where several turtles are kept together it is unnecessary to chop the food into small pieces as the animals themselves will tear it apart by a tug-of-war and claws. This not only exercises them but gives them something to do.

As with the tortoises, it is not advisable to hibernate captive emydid turtles unless one is completely sure of providing the correct conditions. Pet turtles have been known to live many years in captivity even when kept active all year. However, it is probably advisable to feed only about half the normal quantity of food and to reduce the temperature during the winter months — about November to February — at least for species from temperate climates.

Let us now look at some of the species of emydid turtles that may be available and may be kept in the manner described. Any specific requirements will be dealt with in the appropriate section as necessary.

The genus *Pseudemys* contains about 14 species and many subspecies, the most frequently available being the red-ear, *Pseudemys scripta elegans.* The genus is widely distributed from eastern North America through the West Indies (where several island forms exist) and Central and South America as far south as Argentina.

Common Red-eared Turtle, *Pseudemys scripta elegans*

This is the species most commonly exported into Europe. It has a wide range in the United States from Texas and Alabama in the South, north to Ohio and Illinois in the North and East. Its red or orange "ear marking" makes it easily recognizable. It is one of the easier species to keep once it is past its baby stage, and its requirements are standard as already described.

The red-ear is easy to sex, the males having a longer tail and extremely long claws on the front feet; they are usually smaller than females and often much darker. The claws on the front feet are secondary sexual characters and are used during mating display to caress the sides of the female's face. Some red-ear males are so amorous that they will spend hours endeavoring to get in the correct position to stroke their mate's face, but often

Below: *The bright red coloration of the neck and margins of the shell makes the painted turtle,* Chrysemys picta, *an attractive turtle popular with hobbyists. It is often abundant, eats a great variety of foods, and lives well in captivity if given sufficient light for basking.*

with no response at all from their partner.

Yellow-bellied Slider, *Pseudemys scripta scripta*

Sometimes the closely related yellow-belly is available, a few specimens occasionally arriving with consignments of the previous subspecies in European markets. They lack the red coloring on the sides of the head but make up for this by having a larger amount of yellow. The carapace is usually darker but with some yellow showing around the marginals. Its requirements are similar to those of the red-ear.

Painted Turtle, *Chrysemys picta*

A small turtle rarely growing more than 19 cm in length, it is a very attractive creature. The dark brown carapace is often marked with bright red, particularly around the marginals; there are also red stripes on the limbs, and the head and neck are striped in bright yellow. Most of the plastron is a creamy yellow color. It is native to much of the eastern and northern United States and also all along the southern Canadian border. Its requirements are much as for the red-ear.

The next group of turtles is often confused with true tortoises because they are seldom seen in water, but the box turtles *(Terrapene)* are actually emydid turtles that have become almost completely terrestrial and may

be treated much as tortoises, although they need more water and humidity. All of these box turtles have a hinged plastron that enables them to lock themselves tightly into their shells. There are two hardy species found in the United States, plus a few rare species in Mexico and northern Central America.

Eastern Box Turtle, *Terrapene carolina*

Found in the eastern, southern, and central United States, usually in woodland areas, these box turtles vary tremendously in color both individually and according to distribution, but they are all small, with a carapace length rarely exceeding 15-17 cm. All are mainly terrestrial but swamps do not seem to worry them unduly as they commonly overwinter in mud and hatchlings spend their first months in the mud. They are omnivorous and subsist on small insects, molluscs, and some carrion as well as fruits, succulent leaves, and mushrooms. Captive specimens can be fed small pieces of meat as a substitute for their animal prey, but many prefer strawberries, cherries, apples, and other fruits with an occasional meaty treat. Most specimens of eastern box turtles are attractively colored with bright yellow, orange, and dark brown stripes and blotches on the shell and limbs and head.

Above and below: *The eastern box turtle,* Terrapene carolina, *has long been a favored pet. It is colorful, feeds well in captivity on a varied diet, and is long-lived. Many hobbyists prefer to hibernate the species each winter, but others believe this is dangerous.*

Above: *The western box turtle,* Terrapene ornata, *is very similar to the eastern, differing mostly in having a more radiated color pattern. It is kept much like the more familiar species but also does well under drier conditions.*

Western Box Turtle, *Terrapene ornata*

The western box turtle is an attractive species found in the central and southwestern United States, where it prefers sandy areas in contrast to the woodland habitat of the preceding species. It has a rather nice pattern of yellow and dark brown radiating markings on the carapace and plastron, the dark head and limbs being relieved with a speckling of lemon yellow to red.

Map turtles *(Graptemys)* consist of less than a dozen species found in the United States. Several of the species have very restricted ranges and are threatened by pollution and habitat modification.

Common Map Turtle, *Graptemys geographica*

Named after the map-like pattern of yellowish lines on its carapace, this species has extremely broad and strong jaws in old females, which crush the shells of molluscs. Within the genus there is a marked sexual dimorphism, the female usually being twice the size of its male counterpart, averaging 25 and 12.5 cm respectively. It is a very nervous species and normally lives in large lakes and rivers where it can quickly dive deeply should its security be threatened.

False Map Turtle, *Graptemys pseudogeographica*

The false map turtle comes from the central United States. There is a prominent row of knobs down the middle of the carapace in at least juveniles and males, a character typical of most species of the genus. In this species the female again is twice the size of the male, the latter being rarely more than 12 cm.

Mississippi Map Turtle, *Graptemys kohni*

A species frequently available in Europe, the Mississippi map turtle is found from southern Nebraska down to the coasts of Louisiana and Texas. The long crescent-shaped stripe behind and under the eye is distinctive.

Below: *The bright yellow spot behind the eye combined with the saw-toothed back edge of the carapace identify the false map turtle,* Graptemys pseudogeographica. *It requires very clean water.*

Above: *A male black-knobbed map turtle,* Graptemys nigrinoda, *showing the extreme development of the knobs in the middle of the carapace. These knobs are developed in most map turtle species, especially males of the southern species.*

Below: *The Mississippi map turtle,* Graptemys kohni, *is readily identified by the yellow crescent behind the eye. Like other map turtles, it requires clean water and basking facilities to do well in captivity.*

Chicken Turtle, *Deirochelys reticularia* Found in the southern United States, the chicken turtle bears a superficial resemblance to the sliders and painted turtles, but on closer inspection it will be found to have a longer neck, to lack the red coloration, and to be an altogether more elongated animal. The reticulation of many subspecies have been described. It was once considered a delicacy, and at the turn of the century this fact almost led to its complete extinction. It was only the popularity of turtle farming that really saved it, the captive-reared specimens quickly removing the necessity to capture wild stocks. Also, tastes have

Above: *The diamondback terrapin,* Malaclemys terrapin, *is still considered a game animal in much of the coastal eastern United States, so a fishing license may be required to collect it.*

orange-yellow lines on the carapace is fairly distinctive. It is omnivorous and will eat almost anything offered to it in captivity. It derives its common name from the fact that it previously appeared on the menu of Indians and the early settlers and was said to taste like chicken.

Diamondback terrapin, *Malaclemys terrapin* This is another species that is the only one of its genus, though changed and "terrapin" is now seldom served in restaurants. It is an attractive turtle with a light gray, dark spotted skin, orange or white "lips," and often yellow or orange markings on the plastron. The laminae of the carapace are often deeply incised in a regular circular pattern. Being almost entirely carnivorous it will take a variety of animal foods in captivity including fish, meat, snails, and worms. It is

Above: Emys orbicularis, *the common European pond turtle, is a common pet animal in Europe but has never been widely available in the United States.*

confined to brackish waters down almost the entire eastern coast of the United States. In captivity a small amount of salt should be added to its water, otherwise it is likely to succumb to fungus infections. This is one of the few turtles considered a game animal in parts of the United States, its taking being regulated with catch limits and open seasons.

European Pond Turtle, *Emys orbicularis* The genus *Emys* contains only one species, which is distributed over most of central and southern Europe, northern Africa, and the Middle East. It was always one of the more popular species kept as pets in northern Europe, but during the seventies it became increasingly difficult to obtain. Perhaps it has been over-collected in the past or perhaps legislation in its countries of origin has made it more difficult to export. Whatever the reason, it is better that it should be unobtainable in the pet shop rather than become extinct in the wild.

It is normally a dark brown in color with lightish spots. The maximum length is about 18 cm. A very shy creature and very difficult to observe in the wild, it will dive from its basking rock or log at the slightest disturbance. If obtainable, it can conveniently be kept in an outside pen for most of the year although it is not likely to breed in northern climates where the summers are so short.

It is a shame that our turtle-keeping predecessors did not experiment with breeding techniques when the animals were more readily available.

**Blanding's Turtle,
*Emydoidea blandingii*** This semi-aquatic turtle bears a

Below: *The Caspian turtle,* Mauremys caspica, *is another European species that is seldom seen in the United States. It can be kept much like the sliders.*

Above: *The wood turtle,* Clemmys insculpta, *has a reputation as an intelligent, long-lived pet. Its partially aquatic, partially terrestrial habits make it relatively easy to care for. However, it is now protected over much of its range.*

fairly close resemblance to the European pond turtle, but it is quite distinct in skull and shell structure characters. The bright yellow throat and lower jaw combined with hinged plastron are distinctive. It is larger than *E. orbicularis* (up to 26 cm) and is found in the area of the Great Lakes in North America.

Caspian Turtle, *Mauremys caspica* The Caspian turtle is often available in European pet shops. It tends to be more readily available than *Emys orbicularis* and is probably more abundant in its wild haunts. The species ranges from Iran and Arabia to Bulgaria and the Aegean Islands. (A similar species, *M. leprosa,* ranges from Spain to North Africa.) The record length for this species is 25 cm, although 20 cm is a more typical maximum. The carapace is normally an olive-brown with faint markings, the plastron usually black. The head and limbs are usually subtly striped with green and buff. It is another hardy species suitable for the outdoor pen, although it is not likely to breed in northern latitudes unless given artificial sunlight.

Wood Turtle, *Clemmys insculpta* The wood turtle is almost totally terrestrial, extremely intelligent, and rather large (up to 25 cm). It makes an extremely interesting pet and may be kept almost like a tortoise, but a swimming pond must be available for it. The keeled shell is brownish in color, the throat and limbs orangeish, while the head is usually blackish. It is fairly hardy and indigenous to the northeastern United States. Unfortunately, loss of habitat has decreased the numbers of this species and it is now protected in several states.

Spotted Turtle, *Clemmys guttata* A small, attractive species that rarely exceeds 12 cm in total length, the spotted turtle is dark, often almost black in color with large conspicuous yellow spots on the head and on the carapace that seem to increase in number as the turtle gets older (some specimens have almost no spots). It is found in the eastern United States from Maine to northern Florida and is often common.

Japanese Turtle, *Mauremys japonica* The Japanese turtle deserves a brief mention. It rarely exceeds 15 cm in length and is usually drab in color, being dark brown and black.

Tropical Wood Turtles, *Rhinoclemys* This contains some 9 or 10 species in Mexico and Central and South America. Most do not possess a common name in English, but many are extremely colorful and make interesting inmates for the home vivarium. They may possess vivid red stripes on the head, neck, and limbs and sometimes even on the carapace laminae.

Cog-wheel Turtle, *Heosemys spinosa* This unusual turtle occurs in the Malay peninsula and south to Borneo. It has sharp spines at the rear of each costal and marginal lamina, giving it a sort of cog-wheel shape. It is normally a light brown color and grows to a maximum length of almost 20 cm. It is said to be largely vegetarian in its diet, but specimens the author has kept have shown a marked liking for animal foods.

Below: *Close-up of* Rhinoclemys pulcherrima, *a Mexican wood turtle.*

Above: *Cog-wheel turtles,* Heosemys spinosa, *are relatively recent imports on the American pet market, but they have proved to be quite popular. The bizarrely spined carapace margins are unique.*

Above: *The spiny turtle,* Heosemys grandis, *is closely related to the cog-wheel turtle but not so spectacular.*

Below: *When available, Asian box turtles make fine pets. They are kept much like American box turtles but like it a bit wetter. This is* Cuora amboinensis.

Spiny Turtle, *Heosemys grandis* This is the largest species of the genus and is occasionally available on the market. It makes an exceptionally good pet, becoming extremely tame and confiding. Its only drawback is the fact that it grows to 40 cm or more in length, which is much too large for the average living room tank. It is mainly dark brown to black in color and has a prominent ridge along the center of the carapace as well as strong spines on the marginal laminae. It will feed on most types of food normally offered to turtles.

Asian Box Turtles,
Cuora The chapter on emydid turtles could hardly be terminated without mention of the genus *Cuora,* the most popular and often available Asian box turtles. One species in particular is frequently sold as a pet, the Amboina box turtle, *Cuora amboinensis.* This charming little turtle is partially aquatic and is often found in rice paddies in Southeast Asia where it is said to be almost totally vegetarian (one would suspect that they could be accused of eating the young rice shoots). However, captive specimens will readily take meat. The carapace is usually a dark greenish brown in color and there are vivid yellow stripes on each side of the head. The plastron is of a much lighter color.

Below: *A fine specimen of* Cuora trifasciata, *one of the Asian box turtles.*

Snappers, Mud Turtles, and Softshells

As the requirements of these turtles are slightly different from the emydid turtles and less different from each other, they have been placed together in a single chapter, but the three families will be dealt with in separate sections.

Snappers: Chelydridae

There are only two species in this family, each in a different genus.

Alligator Snapping Turtle, *Macrochelys temmincki* The alligator

snapper is so named due to its ferocious appearance and its habit of snapping up its prey; in folklore it also was thought to be the result of an immoral association between a conventional turtle and an alligator.

This species can be described as no less than incredible. It is one of the largest freshwater turtles known, and carapace lengths of over 60 cm have been recorded. Such a specimen may well weigh almost 100 kilograms. It has a very large head and jaws of such power they are easily capable of shearing off a man's fingers or toes. But perhaps the most amazing thing of all about this animal is the worm-like appendage on its tongue that it uses to lure unsuspecting fishes into its cavernous mouth before dispatching them with one gulp into its gullet. The appendage bears an uncanny resemblance to an earthworm, is reddish in color, and even has "segments." Like a worm, it has a wide tail end and a narrower "head" end. It is joined to the tongue by a narrow bridge of tissue at a situation roughly in the center of the worm's body. When fishing, the animal lies motionless on the river bed, its mouth wide open, the only movement being the sinister wriggling of the worm.

The alligator snapper is found only in the United States, ranging from central Texas to Florida and as far

Above: *A close-up of the mouth of the alligator snapping turtle,* Macro-chelys temmincki, *showing the worm-like filament on the floor of the mouth. This filament is actually wriggled to attract small fishes into striking range.*

north as Illinois and Michigan. It is one of the most sluggish of all the chelonians and spends long periods lying in the water doing nothing at all; in fact, algae grow on its shell, providing extremely effective camouflage. In captivity it is no less ravenous than in the wild and will devour almost any animal matter offered to it — including fingers — so be warned. One that was kept by the author for several years would swallow herrings, rats, day-old chicks, mice, and chunks of meat. Any object that is too large to swallow whole is simply sheared in two by the strong, sharp jaws.

One handy point when keeping an alligator snapper is that one always knows when it is hungry, as it lies with its jaws open and wriggles its worm!

Common Snapping Turtle, *Chelydra serpentina* If anything, the common snapper is more ferocious than the preceding species. If

central United States south to Central America and then to Ecuador. It is another hardy and easy to care for species in captivity and will do well on a diet of meat and fish.

Mud and Musk Turtles: Kinosternidae

The mud and musk turtles are generally thought to be rather closely related to the

Above: *Few turtles have a more primitive look than does the common snapping turtle,* Chelydra serpentina. *The long tail with crests on top, the large head, and the ferocious behavior give it a distinctive character. They live forever it seems, but seldom make good pets.*

pulled out of the water onto land it will attack viciously anything that moves near it. It is smaller than the alligator snapper, and specimens more than 35 cm in length are rare; the maximum weight is probably no more than 39 kilograms. It also has a much wider range, being found in the whole of the eastern and

snappers, and in spite of extreme size differences there are many similarities. Four genera are recognized with about 23 species in all, most in the genus *Kinosternon*.

Eastern Mud Turtle, *Kinosternon subrubrum* Most of the mud turtles are capable of

producing a foul smell from their cloacal glands, and the eastern mud turtle is no exception. The smell is usually produced when the animal is in danger, but with time captive specimens usually lose the habit. *K. subrubrum* is probably the most well-known species of the genus and also the species most frequently exported to Europe. It is found over most parts of the southern United States and is usually common in its range. It prefers shallow swampy areas as opposed to deeper water and spends much of its time tramping about in damp vegetation. It is a small species — rarely over 12 cm in length — and the smooth, oval carapace is usually a dark reddish brown.

Striped Mud Turtle, *Kinosternon bauri* Another small species, this turtle is named for the three light stripes along its carapace. It ranges from southernmost Florida to southern Georgia.

Below: *The yellow mud turtle,* Kinosternon flavescens, *is one of the dozen or so mud turtles at least theoretically suitable as pets. Since they are largely nocturnal, burrow in the bottom, and have no personality, however, they are not popular.*

Yellow Mud Turtle, *Kinosternon flavescens*

One of the larger mud turtles, this species may grow up to 16 cm in length. Although called "yellow," the carapace is more likely to be olive or brown in color; it is the chin and neck that are yellow. It occurs from Illinois southwest to Arizona and northeastern Mexico.

Scorpion Mud Turtle, *Kinosternon scorpioides*

There are several races of this turtle found over a colossal range, from southern Mexico to Panama in Central America right down into northern Argentina. The carapace is usually reddish brown and the head is spotted with yellow or red.

The next genus to be discussed is *Sternotherus*, the musk turtles. As their name indicates, they are even more evil-smelling than the previous group and have, in fact, earned such alternative descriptive names as stinkpot and stinkin' Jenny! The odor is emitted from a pair of glands situated in the soft skin adjacent to the thighs. The animal has a rather small plastron with much skin exposed between the laminae and is unable to completely withdraw inside its shell. However, due to its musk glands and rather vicious temper it is unlikely to be set upon by many predators. There are four species of musk turtles, *Sternotherus*

odoratus, S. carinatus, S. minor, and *S. depressus,* all of which occur in the eastern United States.

Stinkpot, *Sternotherus odoratus*

This is the most well-known of the musk turtles and the one most likely to be kept in captivity. It is found throughout all the eastern United States, where it lives in all manner of freshwater ponds, rivers, and lakes. When captured, this species is extremely pugnacious as well as emitting its musk, so it should be handled with care. It is a rather small reptile, never more than 14 cm in length. The smoothly rounded carapace is normally yellowish brown in color. There are two white stripes on either side of its head.

All species in the family Kinosternidae may be treated in the manner recommended for emydid turtles. They tend to be more aquatic than most emydids and more nocturnal, but basking facilities should still be offered.

Softshell Turtles

The softshell turtles can hardly be mistaken for any other group of more conventional chelonians, as all the 20 species lack the usual bony shell of the carapace, this being replaced by a soft leathery skin that in some species is rather attractively colored and patterned, quite unlike the coloring of most other turtles. In the softshells, the snout is elongated so that the animal can breathe without surfacing. The snout accounts for the rather benign but unusual facial expression of all softshells. All species are carnivorous and feed mainly on fishes but also on other aquatic animals and carrion sharp jaws. In the case of a very large fish, the softshell contents itself with just a "bite-sized chunk"; fishes caught by anglers in rivers where softshells occur often sport many scars of such encounters.

Softshells can be rather vicious and will think nothing of removing part of their

Above: *The musk turtles have few advantages over their close relatives the mud turtles, but some people find them more interesting. Shown is* Sternotherus minor, *a southern United States species with a much brighter head pattern than the common stinkpot.*

that falls into the river. They rely on their camouflage, often lying partially submerged in the mud or detritus on the bed of the watercourse when catching food. As an unsuspecting fish swims within range the turtle strikes with lightning speed and catches it in its razor- doting owner's anatomy given half a chance. Tanks containing these creatures should be kept out of reach of young children who may be tempted to stroke the beasts!

Indian Flap-shelled Turtle, *Lissemys punctata* This is one of the smaller species of

Above: *When available, the Indian flap-shelled turtle,* Lissemys punctata, *makes a fine pet. Like many of the other softshell turtles, it is active and has a voracious appetite. Juveniles have a brightly spotted pattern on the head and carapace, but much of this fades as the turtle grows. Like all softshells, it is subject to fungus infections if the ventral shell becomes abraded or cut. It also tends to foul the water rapidly.*

softshell, with an adult length of 20 cm. The domed carapace is olive-green with lemon yellow spots; the plastron (which has large posterior side flaps) is predominantly yellow. It is found throughout the Indian subcontinent and parts of Burma.

Aubrey's Softshell Turtle, *Cycloderma aubryi*
A medium-sized West African softshell with a maximum length of about 36 cm, Aubrey's softshell is mainly yellowish brown in color with a few darker blotches. There are five dark longitudinal lines along the head, which is white under the chin.

Senegal Softshell Turtle, *Cyclanorbis senegalensis*
The maximum length of this species is 30 cm. It is found from the Sudan to West Africa, where it is often used as a food item. The adult carapace is dark green with a white margin; the plastron is much paler in color.

Indian River Turtle, *Chitra indica*
Probably the largest softshell, the Indian river turtle is infamous for its unsavory activities. There are stories of it sinking boats, and this would not be too difficult for a specimen with a reputed length of 180 cm. The more usual (and documented)

Above: *The Florida softshell turtle,* Trionyx ferox, *reaches a large adult size but makes a passable pet when young. It is not exactly attractive, however, and has the same problems that other softshells have—a vicious temper and susceptability to fungus.*

length, however, is about 90 cm. It occurs in the great river systems of the Indian subcontinent and is well known in the Indus and the Ganges. Part of its range extends into the Malay peninsula. It has a rather long neck for a softshell and its head is small, with the eyes set very close to the short snout. The general coloring of the animal is light with a pattern of darker markings.

Antipa Softshell Turtle,
Pelochelys bibroni This species is found in much of Southeast Asia but may even reach as far as New Guinea, where it is found in diverse aquatic habitats ranging from clear streams to brackish estuaries. It is another very large softshell, lengths of over 120 cm having been confirmed.

Malayan Softshell Turtle,
Trionyx subplanus A much smaller species than the preceding one, the Malayan softshell or dogania rarely exceeds 25 cm. It is a southern Asian species with a range covering Burma, Thailand, Malaysia, Indonesia, and the Philippines. It has rather a

Above: *A juvenile Ganges softshell turtle,* Trionyx gangeticus, *showing the four ocelli on the carapace that occur in several Indian softshells.*

Below: *Smooth softshell turtles,* Trionyx muticus, *lack the spiny tubercles at the anterior edge of the carapace that are found in other American softshells. They are usually nocturnal and seldom seen or collected.*

long neck and a large head that is broad at the rear and tapers to a pointed snout. It is mainly dark brown in color with light spots on the head and neck and a few darker blotches on the carapace.

Florida Softshell, *Trionyx ferox* One of the most widely kept softshells is *Trionyx ferox*, which occurs in Florida and in the Okefenokee Swamp. It grows to about 45 cm in length and is mainly

Above: Dermatemys mawi, *the Mexican river turtle, bears many superficial resemblances to softshells although unrelated.*

dark brown in color. In its native habitat it lives in stagnant water unlike most softshells, which live in rivers.

Spiny Softshell, *Trionyx spiniferus* Named for the rubbery "spines" on the carapace, the spiny softshell hardly can be mistaken for any other species. It has an exceedingly large range from southern Canada into northern Mexico. The average adult length is about 30 cm.

Nile Softshell, *Trionyx truinguis* Mention must be made of the only African member of the genus *Trionyx*. It covers most of the continent in most of the river systems and even extends into Syria. It grows to a maximum of 90 cm in length although the majority of specimens are less than half this size.

Several other species of *Trionyx* are found in Asia, where in certain places they have become religious symbols. *Trionyx gangeticus*, for instance, is kept in a large artificial reservoir at Puri in India and is fed and protected by their Islamic worshippers. The turtles manage to maintain their population level by laying their eggs in the banks of the reservoir. Other species that are worshipped in a similar manner include *Trionyx formosus* and *Trionyx nigricans*.

The Sidenecks

About one-fifth of the world's chelonian species belong to the suborder Pleurodira, in which the neck retracts into the shell in a horizontal rather than a vertical plane. This group is said to be more primitive than the Cryptodira, and features such as the fusion of the pelvis to the shell give support to this theory. The majority of the 50 or so species are found in the Southern Hemisphere, in South America, southern Africa, and Australasia. The Pleurodira is divided into two families, the Pelomedusidae and the Chelidae.

Family Pelomedusidae

There are five genera and about 24 species in this family, which is distributed over South America, Africa, and Madagascar.

River Turtle or Arrau, *Podocnemis expansa*

This, the largest living species of the family, may grow to a length of 90 cm. It was once extremely common in the river systems of the Amazon Basin,

Below: *The arrau turtle,* Podocnemis expansa, *used to come ashore on islands in the Amazon by the thousands, but today their herds are reduced to much smaller numbers. The amount of human predation on this species, especially for the eggs, has been tremendous, as has been the habitat destruction in its Amazon home.*

Above: *This hatchling* Podocnemis erythrocephala *shows the distinctive red band on the head mentioned in the scientific name. Few turtles of this genus can be legally imported today.*

but exploitation by man has led to its rapid decline over the past century. The turtles nest on sand banks and may lay up to 120 eggs at a time. These eggs are collected both for food and for oil extraction. The oil was once exported for use as machine oil, but conservation measures have since prevented this. The Amerindians, however, exploit the turtle to a maximum and further protective action is required if the species is not to become extinct.

The other South American members of this genus are considerably smaller, probably not exceeding 35 cm. Some are quite colorful, with red or yellow markings on the head. All have rather flattened, oval shells. Most members of this genus will do fairly well in captivity and will take both animal and vegetable foods. As most of them grow to a fairly large size, however, they are probably more suited to zoological collections or large indoor pools. Because of the threatened states of most species, they are now seldom imported.

Helmeted Turtle,
Pelomedusa
subrufa Probably one of the

most frequently available sidenecked turtles in European pet shops is the helmeted turtle, which is found over most of Africa south of the Sahara. It swims well but spends much of its time basking in the sun. This and members of the next genus are occasionally seen basking on the backs of hippopotamuses. The average size is 15-18 cm in length. The shell is a uniform brown olive in color. Helmeted turtles have a hinged plastron and are able to withdraw completely within their shells.

In captivity it is almost exclusively carnivorous, and it will take most animal-based foods. It appreciates being provided with a heat lamp and will not tolerate cold temperatures for long periods.

African Black Turtle, Pelusios subniger The most commonly available species of the genus and also probably the most widespread, *Pelusios subniger* occurs right across the central part of Africa and also in Madagascar. Like the other species of the genus, the plastron is hinged and the limbs and head can be completely retracted. The carapace is mainly black and there is a central keel. The head and limbs are usually a yellowish brown. Specimens may grow up to 30 cm in length.

Below: *The helmeted turtle,* Pelomedusa subrufa, *requires very warm surroundings and basking facilities. Although easy to keep, it has little going for it except that it represents the sideneck turtles. Certainly its color will never gain it any friends.*

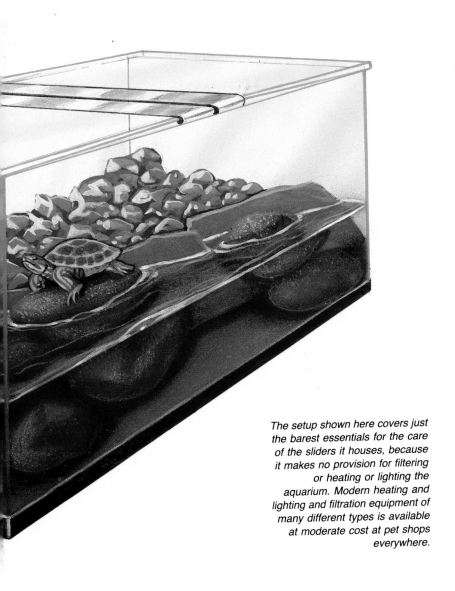

The setup shown here covers just the barest essentials for the care of the sliders it houses, because it makes no provision for filtering or heating or lighting the aquarium. Modern heating and lighting and filtration equipment of many different types is available at moderate cost at pet shops everywhere.

Above: *No, this photo is not retouched—the neck really is this long! This Australian snake-necked turtle,* Chelodina longicollis, *really deserves its name. It is not colorful, but its unusual shape and the facts that it tames readily and does well in captivity make it a popular turtle.*

Family Chelidae

This second family of sidenecked turtles contains 9 or 10 genera and about 35-40 species that are variable in size and form. They are found in South America and the Australian region only. All have rather long necks but some are excessively long.

Australian Snake-necked Turtle, *Chelodina longicollis*

One of the best known *Chelodina* species must be the Australian snake-neck, which, as its name implies, has a neck almost as long as the rest of its body (which may grow to a length of 15-20 cm). It is a rather plainly colored reptile, the head, neck, limbs, and carapace being a uniform olive-brown, while the plastron is dirty yellow. It has very noticeable yellow staring eyes with round pupils. It is common in eastern Australia.

This species is a very popular vivarium inmate and when available makes a most entertaining pet. It quickly becomes tame and will feed from the hand, sometimes standing upright in the water, stretching its neck out, and "begging" in a most comical manner. It will take most animal foods including fish and raw meat.

Two closely related species

are *Chelodina oblonga* from northwestern Australia and *Chelodina expansa* from Queensland. These are somewhat larger than *C. longicollis,* both reaching carapace lengths of 30 cm.

Murray River Turtle, *Emydura macquarrii* This species is probably the most well-known of the Australian turtles, being widely distributed over the southern and western areas of the continent. Unlike the snake-necks *(Chelodina)* that are fairly docile and friendly in captivity, this species can be snappy and inflict a painful bite. Reaching a length of some 32 cm, the reptile is a plain olive brown in color over most of the shell and body.

The carapace is somewhat flattened and there are round, warty protuberances on the neck behind the head.

Krefft's Turtle, *Emydura kreffti* A species that can be distinguished from the Murray River turtle by the yellow lines running from the eye to the ear, Krefft's turtle is found both in New Guinea and northern Queensland.

In South America, the family Chelidae contains four genera, the most famous being *Chelus,* of which there is but a single species.

Matamata Turtle, *Chelus fimbriata* The matamata must be one of the most bizarre of all the world's chelonians. It inhabits slow-

Below: *Not all the Australian snake-necked turtles are actually long-necked. The* Emydura australis *shown here is a very stout-bodied species with a relatively short neck.*

moving and stagnant waters in tropical South America, where it lurks in the mud and leaves on the bottom, relying on its strange warts and tubercles for camouflage as it waits for prey. It has a very large mouth indeed, and when an unsuspecting fish comes too close it is engulfed by a sudden snap of the huge jaws. The matamata grows to a length of 45 cm and requires a large heated aquarium.

Below: *Perhaps one of the most famous turtles is the matamata,* Chelus fimbriata. *This bizarre South American species has irregular projections on the head to help camouflage itself in the debris of the bottom, where it waits for fish and other prey to swim by. When prey comes close enough it suddenly opens the mouth and drops the floor of the mouth, creating a strong water current that actually pulls the fish into the mouth. They seldom do well in captivity.*

Sea Turtles

Above: *Young sea turtles in a large public aquarium.*

It is most unlikely that the readers of this book will ever keep sea turtles in the home as their requirements are far in excess of what the average enthusiast can supply, and of course virtually all species are now protected by law. Even in zoological collections there is little chance that these animals may breed as, due to the complicated migratory cycle of their lives, it is almost impossible to simulate their environment. Exhibits therefore consist of no more than a few adult specimens swimming about in huge saltwater tanks. However, being important members of the chelonian order it is thought that a chapter dealing with these graceful reptiles will not go amiss.

Sea turtles differ from their freshwater counterparts in the way they move through the water. While emydid turtles paddle through the water with alternating motions of their webbed feet, the marine reptiles seem to almost fly through their salty environment, the broad front flippers acting like the wings of a bird. Some sea turtles have been clocked at over 32 kph (20 mph). Rapid turns are engineered by the use of the rudder-like rear flippers.

Virtually all sea turtles are on lists of endangered species of wildlife, as for years they have borne the brunt of man's greed. They make fine soup, the flesh of most species is said to resemble beef, and the eggs

Sea Turtles

Above: *An adult green turtle,* Chelonia mydas, *in shallow water. These once were the favorite turtles for use in turtle soup.*

are such a delicacy in various parts of the world that profiteers will take tremendous risks to procure them even from protected areas. The shells of some species are also valued for ornamental use. Although these reptiles are fast and graceful when in the sea, they become clumsy and vulnerable when on land. It is a well-known fact that turtles must come onto land to lay their eggs, and it is here that the adult female comes under the greatest threat of her life. She will normally laboriously plod up the beach to just above high water mark before excavating a deep hole in the sand with her flippers. The eggs, usually about the size of ping-pong balls, are then laid in the hole before being covered over. Strangely, it is only certain beaches that will do for egglaying. Others that to the human eye would seem perfectly adequate are ignored by the reptiles. It is knowledge by egg-collectors of these special beaches, called "rookeries," that makes protecting them during the laying season an important factor in the conservation of these animals. In some countries where sea turtles nest, conservation volunteers — and even armed soldiers — keep a 24-hour watch on beaches during the breeding season.

In some cases, to protect

Left: *The large flippers and streamlined shell of sea turtles reduce drag while swimming.*

hatching turtles (rarely more than 5 cm in length) from a premature death, the eggs are transported to a "turtle ranch" where they are artificially incubated until they hatch. The young turtles are then reared in large tanks of salt water until they are large enough to be released without danger. A certain percentage of the turtles are kept for commercial use. The argument in favor of this method is that had the eggs been left to run their natural course, considerably more of the young turtles would have been destroyed by predators. It is estimated that some 98% of all naturally hatched turtles are destroyed by predators within a week of hatching — one reason why mother turtle lays so many eggs.

There are two families of marine turtles: the Cheloniidae, which contains four genera and seven species; and the Dermochelyidae, containing only one genus and one species. Let us take a brief look at the different species in a little more detail.

The Loggerhead, *Caretta caretta* The genus *Caretta* contains only one species, the loggerhead, so named because of its broad head. It is normally a reddish brown color. Loggerheads are very large reptiles reaching lengths of about a meter and weights of up to 200 kg. Weights of up to 545 kg have been given but are probably erroneous. They have a reputation for being particularly aggressive and many a seaman can tell of frightening experiences with these turtles. Boats have been overturned and savage bites have been inflicted. It must be pointed out, however, that in most of these cases man himself has instigated the episodes by endeavoring to capture or kill the sea turtles. Loggerheads are mainly carnivorous, the main part of their diet consisting of molluscs, crustaceans and other marine invertebrates. They are probably the hardiest of sea turtles. In the Atlantic, they have been found as far north as Scotland and as far south as the Rio de la Plata in Argentina. They nest

Sea Turtles

Above: *The hawksbill turtle,* Eretmochelys imbricata, *is probably the most attractive species of the group, with the brightly variegated scutes being valuable at one time for the production of tortoiseshell jewelry.*

on subtropical to temperate beaches where they lay 120-150 eggs that take 35-65 days to hatch.

Green Turtle, *Chelonia mydas* The oval shell of this species is characterized by the smoothness of the laminae which are closely knit and do not overlap. It is usually a dark olive-green in color although not necessarily so — some specimens are brown or almost black. The green turtle is found in seas throughout the tropics but, for some obscure reason, it nests up to 2,000 kilometers away from its feeding grounds and a complex system of breeding and feeding migrations has evolved. Scientists are still puzzled as to precisely how the turtles can navigate to

remote nesting beaches, some on very small islands.

As green turtles are largely vegetarian, they congregate in large numbers to browse upon turtlegrasses, green marine plants that grow in beds in the shallow tropical waters. They also take certain algae and some invertebrates. They are a large species, and individuals with a carapace length of 1.40 m have been recorded; reports of specimens up to 450 kg in weight cannot be discounted, although the official maximum is about 300 kg.

Hawksbill, *Eretmochelys imbricata* Named for their narrow, hooked beaks, hawksbills are found in the Atlantic and the Indo-Pacific. Unlike the green turtle, the

Above: The leatherback turtle, Dermochelys coriacea, *is undoubtedly the largest of the sea turtles although its actual size has been considerably exaggerated over the years. Now that it is fairly well known it has lost some of the aura of mystery that once surrounded it. One of its major problems today is that it tends to confuse floating plastic garbage bags with the jellyfish on which it normally preys; the plastic bags clog the intestines and result in death.*

carapace laminae are thick, rough, and often overlapping. It is a small species, specimens of over 90 cm in length or weighing over 100 kg being rare.

This species is also exploited by man, not so much for food but for the "tortoiseshell." The thick laminae, when ground and polished, produce a beautiful translucent multicolored substance that is much in demand for the manufacture of trinkets and jewelry.

The hawksbill is omnivorous and will eat various small sea creatures as well as vegetative matter. It is said to devour jellyfishes and even the poisonous Portuguese man-o-war, which possibly renders the turtle's own flesh distasteful if not inedible.

Ridley Turtles, *Lepidochelys kempi* and *Lepidochelys olivacea*

The former from the Atlantic and the latter from the Pacific, the two species of ridley turtles are the smallest of the sea turtles, the greatest recorded length being 78 cm. Both species are mainly carnivorous, although a certain amount of vegetable matter may be consumed.

Above: Chelonia mydas *returning to the sea.*

Both the eggs and the flesh of the ridleys are eaten in many parts of the range, although the latter is said to be unpalatable. Kemp's ridley is approaching extinction.

Leatherback, *Dermochelys coriacea* The largest of the living turtles and possibly the bulkiest and heaviest of all living reptiles, the leatherback has a family all to itself, the Dermochelyidae. Unlike most other turtles, this species possesses no horny lamellae but has instead a thick leathery skin that is raised in a number of ridges on both the carapace and plastron. The bones of the shell are greatly reduced, especially those of the plastron.

This reptile is circumtropical in distribution and mainly pelagic, living in the midst of the sea rather than on the sea bottom. As medium-sized specimens are rarely seen, it is presumed that they spend their formative years in deep water.

At nesting time the gravid females seek out suitable sites on remote tropical beaches where they laboriously dig holes well over a meter in depth before laying up to 90 eggs. The author has observed the nesting of this species on the well-known beach at Trengganu on the eastern coast of Malaya. Fortunately this site is now protected.

An adult leatherback turtle is mainly black in color but may be lighter on the underside, even a shade of pink. The youngsters are black with yellow or white spots. It is said to be the fastest of all tetrapod swimmers.

90

Specialized Housing

The housing of chelonians can be conveniently divided into three different categories: (i) hardy tortoise accommodations; (ii) tropical tortoise accommodations; and (iii) aquatic turtle accommodations. To a certain extent these categories are interchangeable. For instance, hardy emydids may sometimes be housed in category (i), as also may be tropical tortoises in mid-summer. Also, hardy tortoises may be housed in category (ii) if one does not want to hibernate them for any particular reason.

Category (i): Hardy Tortoise Accommodations

The hardiness of the European and some North American tortoises renders them interesting inmates for the suburban garden, but it is not recommended that they be given a free run as they will soon "disappear." Even a "slow moving" tortoise on a warm day will cover a lot of ground in a couple of hours. Some "lost" tortoises turn up two or three years later, having apparently fended for themselves in the area. However, it is not to be expected that most tortoises

Although an aquarium-type container can be covered to increase humidity, it is of little advantage in keeping tortoises, where humidity is an enemy.

Above: *This pair of adult red-legged tortoises,* Geochelone carbonaria, *have obviously been well cared for. Many of the larger tortoises (and turtles for that matter) can be allowed to run loose in fenced yards during the summer—just make sure they are protected from extremes of temperature and predators.*

will survive a hard temperate winter.

Accommodations for tortoises can vary; it is usually up to individual taste and can also depend on how "fanatical" the tortoise owner is himself. Simple housing for a pet tortoise can consist of a ring of wire netting about 30 cm in height pegged down onto the lawn. A small wooden house can be placed inside this, preferably one with a floor. For a pair of Mediterranean tortoises a house 50 cm long, 30 cm wide, and 25 cm high is ideal. The advantage of this type of enclosure is that it can be regularly moved to fresh pastures. For greater permanency the wire netting may be put into the ground and bent inward to stop the inmate from burrowing out. It is also advisable to bend the wire inward at the top to stop it from climbing over.

The author prefers a much more permanent sort of tortoise pen, one in which other creatures may also be kept, perhaps a few lizards or a combination of tortoises and emydid turtles. This may consist of a concrete block or brick enclosure inside which an attractive landscape can be planned. The amateur handyman can derive a great deal of pleasure from designing and constructing an enclosure for his tortoises. Let us look at the type of pen one can construct. The design shapes and measurements given are, of course, only guidelines and will depend on the personal taste of the enthusiast, the type of species to be kept, and the available space.

The Tortoise Rockery For three or four pairs of hardy tortoises, an enclosure some 5 meters by 2.5 meters would be ideal. First mark out the shape of the enclosure, preferably on level ground, and dig out a trench about 20 cm wide and 20 cm deep. With the use of wooden pegs and a spirit level make sure that you have correct levels all around before filling the trench with concrete made from 4 parts sand, 3 parts gravel, and 1 part cement.

Below: *Indian starred tortoises,* Geochelone elegans, *seem to be quite subject to pneumonia or a similar respiratory disease. With many tortoises the major problem in keeping them is trying to control the humidity.*

93

Above: *This hinge-backed tortoise,* Kinixys homeana, *is doing well in a native garden.*

Smooth out the concrete to the top of the level pegs and allow at least 24 hours for it to dry out before continuing.

The most practical and simple materials for building the wall are concrete blocks, but more attractive reconstituted stone blocks are also available. These are cemented together using a mortar of 1 part cement to 4 parts sand. For most tortoises a wall 45 cm high is ample, but if you intend to keep other reptiles in the enclosure such as snakes or terrestrial lizards the wall will have to be at least 100 cm high and also have an overhang to prevent some of the little sharp-clawed inhabitants from escaping. Alternatively, a 15-cm-wide band of glossy laminate (such as Formica) screwed 15 cm down from the top of the wall will prevent these creatures from gaining a foothold.

The inside of the wall should be rendered as smooth as possible with a mixture of 4 parts sand to 1 of cement and a plasticizing additive. This should be applied with a plastering trowel. Allow a couple of hours for the cement to semi-harden before smoothing over with a wooden float. With a little practice it is surprising how soon one can master this process, but anyone who thinks he cannot do it should enlist the help of a friend or acquaintance who can.

The outside of the wall can be either rendered the same as the inside or pieces of flat stone may be stuck onto it with mortar to provide an attractive "crazy paving" effect.

Once the outside wall has been constructed we can concentrate on the landscaping of the inside, and with a little imagination an extremely attractive exhibit can be made.

First of all draw a large plan of the area and fill in the most important parts such as house, pool, rockery, etc. Juggle these about until you are sure where you want them to be, because in a permanent structure such as this it will be too late to change your mind once it has been constructed unless you do not mind another great deal of time and expense. The house itself can be built within a rockery or it can be built into one of the outside walls and incorporate an observation window and heating. The size of the house will depend on the number of tortoises being kept and, to a certain extent, on the precise purpose of it. It may either be used as summer sleeping quarters only or as permanent quarters. The enclosure could be built onto the end of the greenhouse that the tortoise could use for sleeping as well as winter quarters.

As an example we will discuss the construction of a house to be used as sleeping quarters for our 8 tortoises. First a mound of earth is made in the enclosure at the spot where we want the house. The mound can be up to 1 meter in height. The mound is well pressed down before the center is dug out. We will need enough dug out to take a wooden sleeping box about 60 cm long, 45 cm wide, and about 30 cm high. As a base, an 8-cm-thick layer of concrete is laid and the box, with the door facing outward, is placed on this. The cavity between the box and the earth may then be filled with proofed concrete, and a removable concrete slab may be placed on the roof in case it is necessary to get at the contents at any time. Earth is then piled around the whole thing and a pleasing effect can be made by embedding rocks, using rock plants and turf, while a ramp is made up to the door. A shallow pond may be constructed using waterproofed concrete on a hardcore base.

Category (ii): Tropical Tortoise Accommodations

As in the previous section, many factors must be taken into consideration when constructing a terrarium for tropical chelonians: available space, available cash, type, size and number of species, etc., must all be thoroughly investigated before a decision is made. Only guidelines can be given here, but it is hoped that the enthusiast will be able to pick up enough ideas from these to suit his own particular requirements.

With tropical species heating is of prime importance and, in the case of the desert-dwelling species, it *must* be a dry heat, while with a forest-dwelling species a more humid atmosphere is required. There are various types of heaters available and it is interesting to seek out the one most suitable for your requirements.

For some small tropical tortoises a glass tank heated with a light bulb will suffice as long as the inmates also get some natural sunlight at suitable times of the year. One can experiment with various wattages until the correct daytime temperature is reached. It is recommended that the light bulb be placed at one end of the tank only so that there is a variation in temperature should the animals wish to cool off at any time.

As an example, the author has found that a suitable daytime temperature for species like pancake tortoises, *Malacochersus tornieri,* and starred tortoises, *Geochelone elegans,* can be as much as 35°C (95°F) in the hotter part of the cage but the cooler part should then be no hotter than 25°C (77°F). At night the heat may be completely removed and the animals will be happy at room temperature provided it does not drop below 12°C (54°F). This, in fact, is precisely what happens in many desert environments, the night temperature being considerably colder than the corresponding daytime temperatures.

In addition to a light bulb for heating, a broad-spectrum fluorescent light is also beneficial to a tortoise's health, and it is recommended that such a light is turned on for about four hours per day when it is in close proximity to the animals, as in a small tank. The ultra-violet rays emitted from these lights are a substitute for those from actual sunlight (but of course never quite as efficient). At night the lighting and heating must be turned off. One should aim for a cycle of 12 hours of heat and light and 12 hours without. The electronics enthusiast can devise a fully automatic system of time switches, dimmers, thermostats, humidifiers, etc,. to emulate almost any tropical climate he requires.

The Tortoise Table One of the most attractive ways of displaying tortoises indoors is on a tortoise table. This basically consists of a large board (an old table would do admirably) with vertical sides some 25-40 cm wide attached to the edges to stop the tortoises from falling off. One must ensure that the perimeter planks are just higher than the tortoises can reach, otherwise they may clamber out and injure themselves. For more convenient viewing, one of the sides can consist of a piece of plate glass or Plexiglas beveled on the top edge to prevent injury. The best position for a tortoise table is near a south-facing window, thus providing the inhabitants with the benefit of some sunlight. The main source of heat in this kind of enclosure will be infra-red heat lamps. It is possible to obtain infra-red lamps that give off a white light, and these are the most suitable for our purpose. They are hung in their aluminum reflector/shades about 30 cm over the surface of the table allowing the tortoises to bask as little or as much as they wish.

This type of exhibit can be made an extremely attractive feature in a room and may incorporate an indoor garden, a collection of cacti, or just a few pots of colorful plants. Any pots must be securely fixed so that the tortoises cannot knock them over and eat the plants; also pots and there are no holes in the base or joints of the table that will allow the gravel to fall out and make a mess. It is advisable to have two complete lots of gravel available, one lot in use on the table while the other

Above: Geochelone chilensis *would be an excellent addition to the tortoise table if you could control the humidity well enough. Although not really an attractive species, it is quite sturdy and feeds well if the climate is kept dry enough and warm enough. This species, seldom imported, is quite variable in size, general appearance, and color, which has led to the naming of several similar species. Some scientists feel that* G. chilensis *is a complex of at least three species.*

troughs must be high enough to stop the animals from reaching the plants or they will not last very long at all.

The best type of material to use on the floor of the tortoise table is pea-sized gravel, but care must be taken to ensure lot is undergoing washing and drying out for changing at intervals of about one month. Provided the droppings are removed on a daily basis, this monthly change should be adequate.

A shallow water dish should

The Tortoise Table

be let into the base of the table to allow the tortoises to bathe as well as drink should they so wish.

The tortoise table is most suitable for the desert-dwelling species, particularly if the room is centrally heated as the atmosphere may tend to be dry. All heating may be

wishes. Do not put any furnishings near the side walls that would allow the inmates to climb out.

An even more attractive and permanent tortoise exhibit can be built into an alcove or bay window or even in a conservatory or greenhouse. The floor of such an exhibit

Above: *Although not really a tortoise (it's a close relative of the sliders just like a box turtle is a modified slider), some of the tropical wood turtles could be kept in humid tortoise tables. This* Rhinoclemys punctularia *from Guyana is very attractive and can do well without access to water—but it would never make it in a desert terrarium.*

removed at night providing the temperature does not drop below 12°C (54°F).

Other furnishings on the tortoise table may consist of a few flat stones and a couple of bizarrely shaped pieces of driftwood or bleached tree root. These will give the tortoises something to clamber over, run around, or hide under to suit their

can, most conveniently, be constructed from concrete, the advantages being that natural looking pools and "scenery" can be built in along with various labor-saving devices. For instance, a standard sink drain can be incorporated into the bottom of the pool, thus substantially simplifying the cleaning.

The spaces available for

Above: *Although box turtles can be kept in a tortoise table, they really do better if given more humidity. After all, they are related to the sliders.*

such a construction will vary tremendously in size from house to house, but let us imagine we have an alcove 2 meters long and 1 meter wide in a corner of our room that we wish to make into a vivarium for tortoises. The first task will be to build a wall on each side of the alcove and a pillar in the center to take the weight of the concrete base. If the floor of the vivarium is going to be 1 meter high (this being an ideal height for observing the inmates from a sitting position), the walls and pillar should be 85 cm high. 15-cm nails may be banged into the existing wall and these may be cemented between the new bricks for added strength.

Allow about 24 hours for the cement to dry before laying a piece of 1.9 meter x 1 meter x 2-cm-thick shuttering ply horizontally across the new walls and pillar. Attach a 15-cm-wide plank of shuttering to the front to retain the concrete. (15 cm thickness is really the minimum if you wish to incorporate a pond into it.) It is very important that this plank is secure as wet concrete is very heavy and will push out at any weak points. Nail it to the base shuttering and prop it with timber from a batten nailed to the floor or from the far walls. Knock a few more 15-cm nails into the side and back walls to help tie in the concrete base.

Make a hole in the base shuttering at the point where you want the deepest part of the pool to be and insert a sink drain, the top of which should be at the level of the bottom of the pool, say 7.5 cm. An "S" bend and drain pipe may be plumbed onto the sink drain from underneath later. Leave the plug in or the concrete will block the drain up. Now fill the prepared area to a depth of 7.5 cm with concrete of the following mixture:

1 part cement, 3 parts gravel, 4 parts sand, and waterproofer to manufacturer's instructions. Now for reinforcement lay wire mesh onto the surface of the concrete already poured (except at the part where the pond is going to be: a good sized pool for a vivarium of these dimensions may be about 30 x 45 cm) and then pour in the remaining concrete up to the level of the top of the retaining shuttering before smoothing the surface over with a trowel. Do not worry if the pool is filled in at this stage as it will be scraped

out later when the concrete has had a couple of hours to set. Carefully scoop this out until you find the top of the sink drain, mold the pool to its correct shape, and then brush on a paste of 1 part cement to 1 part silver sand in water so that you have a smooth waterproof finish to your pond. This coat will be found to be much more permanent if applied while the concrete is not quite set but hard enough to be brushed on without moving it. The sides of the pool should be made to slope gently to the deepest point so that the tortoises can easily get in and out without a struggle. If one wishes to use gravel on the cage floor, it is a good idea to make a lip of cement about 1 cm high all around the pool to stop the gravel from falling into the water.

At the rear of the vivarium one or two artificial caves and "cliff faces" may be built by cementing natural stones together. Cavities for plant containers may also be molded in, ensuring they are out of reach of the inmates. For the sake of hygiene to ensure there are no small crevices left that may harbor parasites, the whole rockwork may be "painted" with the aforementioned mixture of cement and silver sand to which an appropriate cement coloring has been added. By the careful selection of different colors and careful brushing, a most natural looking smoothish surface will be created that will remove the effect of rocks being cemented together and appear like one whole rock face.

If the exhibit is to be left open-topped, a painted or polished piece of timber should be placed to cover the unattractive front edge of the concrete base and doors may be fixed over the cavity below to provide useful cupboard space. A removable 25-cm glass or Plexiglas strip should be fixed along the front edge to stop the animals from falling out, and special grooved frames can be made to take this (it may be possible to have a frame welded locally).

Alternatively, particularly if you are keeping species requiring a more humid environment, it may be necessary to encase the whole exhibit within a glass-fronted cabinet. This means, of course, that a roof and glass paneled doors must be fitted, which should pose no great problems for the handyman. Another advantage of the enclosed exhibit is that heat is retained more efficiently and the ceiling provides fixing points for heaters, lamps, etc.

A good method of maintaining high humidity in a cage is to pass air into the pool via an airstone and a small aerator of the type used

Below: *This geometric tortoise,* Psammobates geometricus, *from South Africa requires a very dry environment. Watch out for drafts, which lead to respiratory problems.*

in fish tanks. If the pump is outside the vivarium, it will also provide a certain amount of ventilation as well as moisture in the air. To further promote humidity an aquarium heater controlled by a thermostat can also be kept in the pool. A final word about tortoise accommodations is that if you are lucky enough to have a spare room the whole area could be used for keeping tortoises. Again, one can place heat lamps in positions where the reptiles can bask under them, but be sure to avoid drafty places.

Category (iii): Aquatic Turtle Accommodations

The simplest form of aquatic turtle accommodation is a plain glass tank containing a light bulb and a basking rock. Perhaps this is one of the best ways to keep most aquatic or semiaquatic turtles of the emydid type, but there are species that are more or less aquatic and their accommodations must be adjusted accordingly.

Basically, most turtles will thrive in habitats developed for tortoises, but with the addition of varying amounts of

Below: *For most turtles, especially sliders and their relatives, the aquarium should contain both water and land. At the very least, there must be access to basking areas, usually wooden platforms or sheets of cork. Basking is very important for most aquatic emydid turtles, and many cannot survive without basking in the sun or a convincing substitute.*

Above: *This baby slider,* Pseudemys concinna, *will need lots of calcium in its diet if it is to grow. This can be provided by calcium supplements in its food or as turtle blocks of special gypsum. A varied and very nutritious diet will also be a must, as will warm, clean water and sufficient light for basking.*

water, depending on the species. Some of the more aquatic species like snappers and softshells only come onto land to lay their eggs, so unless breeding is anticipated these may be kept almost exclusively in water.

In order to avoid too frequent changing of the water, which can upset some species, a filtration system may be installed. There are several types of filters on the market, but they are usually some variant on a box or cylinder containing a filter medium through which water is forced by a pump before being returned to the tank. The undergravel filters often used in both marine and freshwater fish tanks are unsuitable for turtles, particularly softshells, as they are continually turning over the gravel and destroying the filter effect.

Indoor Turtle Pool An attractive method for displaying some of the more tropical turtles is to construct an indoor pool that may become a delightful focal point in a hall or covered patio. There is no limit to the kinds of materials one may use in pool construction, ranging from a plastic child's wading pool to carved marble, but guidelines are given here using red house bricks.

Imagine we have a stretch of blank wall in front of which we wish to construct a semicircular or rectangular or any shape turtle pool. The size, of course, will depend on the amount of available space, but it should be made as large as possible, in this case 3 meters along the wall and 1.5 meters out. A semicircular wall is built from ordinary red building bricks onto a solid concrete floor (it is no use contemplating such a scheme on a timber floor). If the finished pool is to be above 30 cm deep, five courses of bricks should suffice. On top of the wall 15-cm-square red tiles are cemented with an overhang of 5 cm over the pool to prevent the escape of the inmates. At the back of the pool another semicircular wall is built to contain the island on which the turtles may bask or even lay eggs if the facilities are provided. The diameter of this can be about one meter The front margin can be about 20 cm wide with the rear part left hollow to contain sand for breeding purposes.

Various cavities can be built into the construction at intervals to contain potted plants that will greatly enhance the whole appearance. Over the island at the rear a heat lamp for basking can be fixed behind a specially constructed cover that can be made of metal or even concrete.

The whole of the lining of the pool should be rendered with at least 1 cm of cement plaster consisting of 1 part cement, 3 parts sand, and waterproofer to the manufacturer's instructions. The layer on the bottom of the pool may be made thicker while the thickness may peter out altogether at the top of the wall. When it is dried out, the cement lining to the pool should be first primed and then a good quality pond sealing compound should be brushed on. It is recommended that a "non-aggressive" color be used for this purpose, "stone" being a favorite. The pool should then be tested for leaks, and it may be found necessary to use 1 or 2 more coats of sealer before it is completely proofed.

Before being used, the pool should be filled and allowed to stand for 24 hours, after which it should be emptied and rinsed, then refilled for stocking. The pool will probably have to be cleaned out at least once a week if it is to remain smell-free, but this will not be too difficult if you have fitted a drain, as you only have to let out the water, scrub the base, and then refill.

Most turtles will get used to this periodic cleaning providing it is done on a regular basis. Disinfectants should never be used, but bleach may be used for scrubbing down, taking care not to splash the turtles with the full-strength fluid. The bleach should be completely rinsed away before refilling the pool with water.

With a little more expense, the addition of a filtration system incorporating a waterfall and even heating may be added, thus reducing the frequency of cleaning out to even bimonthly intervals. There are, as previously mentioned, many kinds of filters and pumps available, and it is beyond the scope of this book to include all of them here. Once more, it must be stressed that turtle accommodations are a personal matter and much individual design must be encouraged; only guidelines are given here.

Below: *The new automatic water changers may be worth experimenting with when keeping aquatic turtles. Turtles are notoriously dirty animals, and constant water changes are required to keep their water clean.*

Health and Hygiene

Above: *This healthy looking* Pseudemys scripta elegans *appears to be at least half grown yet it has a sturdy shell and bright red ear. When raising small emydid turtles one of the major problems is preventing soft shells due to lack of calcium in the diet and light from basking to help convert the calcium into bone in the shell.*

The words health and hygiene go hand in hand. Good health may be defined as a state of physical and mental well-being that manifests itself in stamina, determination, and "joie de vivre," while hygiene is the science of the prevention of disease. Any animal that is diseased cannot be in good health. Where any animal is kept in captivity under potentially stressful conditions, the science of hygiene is as important as the health of the animal itself. Remember that an animal under stress is more susceptible to disease than one that is "happy," so one of the first principles of hygiene is to provide all the animal requires to prevent stress.

In order to carry out good hygienic measures in keeping turtles, it is advisable to understand the types of disease from which a turtle can suffer. As a turtle is a ectothermic reptile, it will suffer mainly from reptilian diseases and is not likely to succumb to the more common endothermic mammalian complaints such as influenza in man or distemper in dogs.

In all animals there are two main categories of disease or ill health. The first is *noncommunicable* conditions that cannot be transmitted from animal to animal, including such things as physical injuries, malnutrition, frostbite, burns, etc. Most noncommunicable conditions are easily preventable by removing the source of the possible damage or providing the correct conditions to alleviate the trouble. The second category of diseases includes those that are *communicable,* those conditions that are transmissible from animal to animal as they are caused by various forms of living organisms ranging from viruses to arthropod parasites.

The means by which infectious organisms are transmitted from one animal to the other can be called the "route." There are four different routes, as follows:

1) Airborne, in which the diseases are usually respiratory and the pathogenic organisms are spread through the air after being discharged from the respiratory tract through coughing, sneezing, and merely breathing.

2) Excremental or enteric, in which the pathogenic organisms are evacuated by the sick animal before being digested by the healthy animal.

3) Arthropod-borne, in which the disease organisms are transmitted by a secondary host such as a tick or a mosquito. The organisms are usually injected during the bite of a blood-feeding vector.

4) Contact, where disease is transmitted directly from one infected animal to the other. These are less common than the other group and include such things as venereal infections.

Most communicable diseases can be controlled by breaking or removing the "route." Airborne infections can be avoided by preventing overcrowding, by providing adequate ventilation, and by quarantining new arrivals. Excremental diseases can be prevented by keeping the turtles' quarters scrupulously clean, by providing fresh drinking water at all times, and by providing clean, wholesome foods. Arthropod-borne infections can be avoided by removing the external parasites from the animals, but contact infections are more difficult to prevent. The secret is to spot the sick animal before it has a chance to infect the others.

Careful observation is, of course, the most essential skill to acquire in order to observe ill health in a chelonian. The keeping of

Parasites

records is also important, and the following points should be carefully noted:

(a) When did it enter hibernation?

(b) When did it emerge from hibernation?

(c) What is its body weight? Is the weight increasing or decreasing?

(d) Is it eating? What is it eating and how much? Is it drinking?

There are few general signs that turtles show when they are ill, but the time that most sickness occurs is during the spring when they emerge from hibernation.

Post-hibernation Problems
When turtles emerge from hibernation their eyelids are often stuck together. The head must be held firmly behind the occipital condyles (where the head joins the neck) and the eyes thoroughly bathed with a boric eye wash solution on a cotton ball.

When turtles come out of hibernation they should be offered warm water to drink in a large shallow dish. They may refuse to feed immediately, but remember that they will not eat until they are thoroughly warm, with a body core temperature of about 23-26°C (73-79°F).

If they still refuse to eat it is advisable to examine the inside of the mouth, as ulcers and infectious stomatitis are unfortunately common and very serious. A veterinarian can make a positive diagnosis of these problems, but it then

will be necessary to force-feed the turtle with fluids and semi-liquid food. Ulcerative or necrotic glossitis occurs commonly in turtles that have hibernated. On emerging, the reptile neither eats nor drinks because of the sore mouth. The beak must be opened before the extent of the lesion on the tongue and other tissues of the mouth can be seen. These turtles are very seriouslly ill and it is necessary to enlist the help of a veterinarian who will clean away the necrotic material, take a swab for bacteriological culture, and help with rehydrating and supplementary feeding. Fluids and mineral replacement are the lifesaving home nursing that must be done regularly and for several months as reptilian tissues are very slow to heal.

Some turtles on emerging from hibernation are constipated. A warm water cloacal irrigation can be most helpful. Some owners find that merely giving their turtle a warm (26°C, 79°F) bath helps empty the cloaca.

Let us now deal with some of the more common diseases that may occur at any time of the year.

Parasites

1) Internal Parasites The common intestinal roundworm of turtles is *Angusticaecum* (these are worms specific to reptiles and will not infect humans). These

Above: *A two-headed slider,* Pseudemys scripta. *This condition is usually due to an accident affecting the egg and partially dividing it into two incomplete embryos early in development, much as in human Siamese twins. Although rare, the condition is fairly well known and is not fatal if it is possible for the turtle to get constant attention.*

are commonly excreted during the month before hibernation when the turtle is emptying its intestinal tract. Do not give a vermifuge at this time; the correct time to treat turtles for worms is during the spring and summer. Be careful which anthelmintic you give your turtle as it will remain in the intestine for 4 weeks. If you give an anthelmintic drug that is absorbed by the intestinal mucosa it will not be present to kill the worms in the lower intestine and, as all anthelmintic drugs are protoplasmic poisons, you will be poisoning some of the living cells in the turtle. There are some modern anthelmintic drugs that are only minimally absorbed from the intestine. The dose of all drugs must be carefully measured out and will vary with the weight of the animal.

Protozoan flagellates can multiply rapidly and do so to excess in some debilitated turtles. These reptiles are observed to be drinking excessively and passing large volumes of wet cloacal excretions that are teeming with millions of microscopic flagellates and could quickly infect other turtles. There are drugs to treat this condition; a veterinarian can confirm the diagnosis and dispense the drug. Other bacterial and viral infections of the alimentary system can frequently be cured using drugs supplied by the veterinarian.

2) External Parasites Newly imported turtles are often inflicted with ticks, large ugly arachnid parasites that lodge themselves between the scales of the limbs or on the soft tissues of the neck and tail regions. The ticks feed on the blood of the reptiles and attach themselves securely by their mouthparts, becoming difficult to remove. The best way is to dab each tick with a little alcohol or petroleum jelly in order to make it loosen its grip and then remove it gently with a pair of tweezers, making sure not to leave the mouthparts in to fester. Application of an antibiotic powder to the wound may be wise.

Mites can also be a problem, particularly in indoor vivaria. They are often difficult to detect as they are rarely larger than a pinhead and do not attach themselves permanently as the ticks do. They normally operate at night and hide in cracks and crevices during the day. They are fairly easy to destroy by hanging a piece of plastic-based insecticide strip in the cage for three to four days.

Occasionally blowflies (bluebottles) lay their eggs on the skin of box turtles and tortoises, especially if the skin is dirty or has a wound. The eggs hatch into larvae (maggots) and the lesion is known as "fly-blown." Should this occur, clean out the maggots and dress the raw ulcerated wound with an antibiotic powder. Keep the turtle indoors away from flies until the wound has healed.

Respiratory Diseases
Certain respiratory diseases caused by organisms multiplying in the respiratory tract can be extremely infectious and dangerous in turtles. Some owners have found this out the hard way when a friend asks them to look after another tortoise or two while they are away on holiday. After the friend returns home and takes his tortoises away, the kind-hearted person who has looked after them notices that many of his own tortoises have developed rhinitis (watery secretion from the nostrils).

If treated at this early stage by taking the infected tortoise indoors into a warm pen and applying a thin smear of mentholated petroleum jelly on the underside of the mandibles (lower jaw), tortoises respond well and the infection is less likely to spread.

In neglected cases

Above: *The very odd appearance of the shell of this old specimen of the Aldabra giant tortoise,* Geochelone gigantea, *seems to be a result of some dietary deficiency in captivity. Many captive tortoises and some turtle specimens raised in captivity almost always have oddly shaped scutes on the carapace, either irregular, deeply divided, or even strongly conical. The exact cause is unknown, but it seems of little concern to the animal.*

secondary bacteria gain entry, bubbles of mucus get blown from the nostrils and block them, and the tortoise starts mouth breathing. If the infection passes down the trachea to the lung pneumonia occurs. The diagnosis of pneumonia can only be made by the veterinarian. Aquatic turtles are just as susceptible to pneumonia as tortoises.

Abscesses

Abscesses usually develop when pathogenic organisms enter a wound and multiply.

Swellings on the head in the region of the eardrum are often abscesses of the inner ear. Because the turtle retracts its head these must be treated under general anesthetic, so it must be dealt with by a veterinary surgeon. More normal abscesses can be drained and packed with antibiotics.

Fungus Infections

Turtles, in particular softshells, are susceptible to fungus infections, the first signs of which are white, feathery growths on the skin or shell. Bathing in a strong saline solution may be helpful, but various chemical treatments such as tincture of iodine, methylene blue, gentian violet, malachite green, etc., may be used under the instructions of a veterinarian. Various preparations manufactured for the treatment of fungal infections in fish and available in pet shops may be used with some effectiveness.

Physical Injuries

Various factors contribute to physical injuries of chelonians. Tortoises are often tethered by one of their hind legs in the country of capture, resulting in lacerations of the scales. Dogs may chew at the shells and cats may attempt to claw the head and legs out of the

of injury (most usually leading to death) is that which occurs when the turtle is accidentally run over by a lawn mower.

Recent advances in veterinary surgery allow the vet to rebuild areas of shell and mend broken limbs, although you may have to look hard to find a vet who will undertake the task. While on the subject of shells, under no circumstances should a hole be drilled in the posterior marginals in order to tether the tortoise with a string. The shell contains living tissue and any such injury will cause pain plus the risk of

shell. Fractured shells may occur when the reptiles are run over by vehicles, have heavy objects dropped onto them, or they are dropped onto hard surfaces. A common but unpleasant form secondary infection. Tortoises and box turtles occasionally hide under piles of refuse that are to be burned, so whenever you have a bonfire check the whereabouts of your pet.

Disease research in turtles has been somewhat neglected in the past, but lately a few dedicated pathologists, zoologists, and veterinarians are making major breakthroughs in this science that we hope will result in an ever-increasing success rate in the treatment of turtle diseases in the future.

This hatching box turtle is typical of most hatchling turtles in that it closely resembles the parents. The shell of the egg is slit open by a sharp egg tooth on the tip of the upper jaw, the baby turtle rotating within the shell. Often baby turtles stay in the opened egg for hours or even days before venturing out to face the world.

Captive Reproduction

The captive reproduction of turtles is a subject that requires a great deal of research, preferably in the country of origin of the reptiles in question. Without research and without a concerted breeding program the time may come when tortoises and aquatic turtles as pets are a thing of the past. One cannot expect to continually remove these reptiles from the wild to provide specimens. There must come a time when there are just no more available.

Courtship and Mating

Different species, of course, have different breeding habits that are closely interlinked with the climate of the habitat, but all species rely on the warmth of the sun's rays (and sometimes decomposing vegetation) to hatch their eggs. The eggs are usually buried in a spot that will provide exactly the correct conditions to hatch the eggs, and there is no better judge of the correct spot than the mother turtle.

The main problem in breeding turtles in captivity seems to be initially getting the animals into breeding condition. One way of doing this is to study the climate of the area where the animals exist in the wild and try to emulate the conditions that prevail during wild mating activity. The different habitats of the many species result in varied stimuli necessary to bring the animals into a

Below: *So far as known (and it is unlikely that any exceptions will be discovered), all turtles lay their eggs in the sand or soil and then cover them with more soil. There is no parental care as such. Unlike bird eggs, the shells of turtle eggs are leathery and flexible and seldom hard enough to be cracked. In many cultures turtle eggs are considered excellent food and may form a large part of the protein in the native diet.*

mating mood. With the European tortoises it seems to be the increased length of daylight and the warmth of the spring sun after the winter period of low activity that trigger the release of hormones into the bloodstream resulting in frenzied mating activity. Again, courting procedures vary from species to species, but in *Testudo graeca* and *Testudo hermanni* courting consists of the males battering the shells of the females with the anterior part of the carapace. The male

Coupling takes place by the male clambering on the back of the female from the rear and thrusting his tail under hers. The tail of the male is often much longer than that of the female in most species for that very reason. The penis is extruded from the vent under the tail and maneuvered into a position for entry into the female's vent, which is in a corresponding position on the

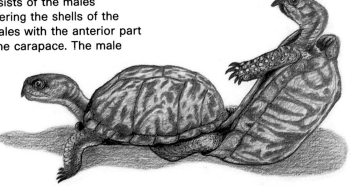

These mating box turtles are in a position fairly common in terrestrial turtles and tortoises, the male standing almost erect behind the female. The bright red eye tends to distinguish the male box turtle from the female, which usually has an orange to brown eye.

does this by planting his feet firmly on the ground and moving his shell (usually with head withdrawn) energetically in the direction of the female in order to attract her attention. Should this fail, the male then proceeds to bite the legs of the female. The procedure can be quite violent, and the female initially attempts to get away at quite a speed. Pieces of flesh are quite often bitten cleanly from the female's limbs by the male. Eventually she will give up and allow him to mate with her.

underside of the tail. The male plastron is usually concave

Egg-laying takes place some 8 weeks after mating. The female excavates a hole in some suitable spot with her hind feet before depositing her eggs. The number and size of the eggs vary from species to species, but the European tortoises usually lay from 2 to 8 eggs that are about 3 cm in length.

Incubation of Eggs
Eggs laid outdoors in temperate climates will not develop naturally, and the

115

chances of their hatching in such conditions are minimal unless an unusually long and hot summer occurs. In latitudes considerably higher than the reptile's natural habitat, the sun's rays are normally too weak and not of sufficient duration to provide the constant temperatures required for embryo development, which normally takes 6-10 weeks depending on the species and the conditions. The main criterion leading to success in the hatching of the eggs of chelonians is the provision of the correct temperature and humidity. Successful hatchings have occurred with the minimum of equipment, and the author has received many reports of tortoises being successfully incubated in ventilated cupboards. The best type of incubation medium for this method seems to be vermiculite chips, which have the advantage of being inert and will retain small amounts of moisture as well as allow air circulation around the eggs. Sand, sand and peat, dried sphagnum moss, absorbent paper tissues, cotton wool, and even plain garden loam have all, however, been used with varying degrees of success.

Always keep close observation on your chelonians as egg-laying time approaches so that you can be sure of the nesting site chosen. Tortoises are very clever at concealing their eggs and, if you do not observe oviposition, there is a chance that the eggs will be lost and there will then be little chance of their hatching.

Allow the female to finish laying and cover the nest site before collecting the eggs. Remove the topsoil carefully and endeavor to keep the eggs in the position in which they were laid. This can be accomplished by gently marking the uppermost side of each egg with a wax crayon. The eggs are placed in the incubation medium with the mark uppermost and are buried just below the surface. Plastic margarine tubs or small cardboard boxes are ideal containers for the incubation material. If an incubator is not available, it is quite possible to use a ventilated cupboard, as long as the temperature is maintained around 30°C (86°F). Occasionally the surface of the medium should be lightly sprayed with water to ensure a reasonable humidity. Care should be taken not to waterlog the medium as this will prevent oxygen absorption through the egg shells.

Unlike the eggs of birds, those of chelonians should never be turned and, once placed in position in the incubation medium, should not be disturbed until hatching time. Needless to say, regular inspections should be made after the fifth week to see if hatching has occurred.

For a greater degree of

Above: *Hatchling turtles have a distinct umbilical scar on the posterior midline of the plastron that represents where they were connected with the yolk sac. Although the last remnants of yolk are used by hatching or within a day or two of hatching, the scar is usually prominent and readily recognized. With growth, the umbilical scar (actually a small opening between the plastral scutes) will disappear.*

success in hatching chelonian eggs, the use of an incubator is highly recommended. A small incubator of the type used by aviculturists can be used with a few modifications, or it is quite simple to construct your own. The latter can consist of a wooden box with a glass door at the front and a few ventilation holes drilled in the sides and the top. The heater can consist of a 100-watt light bulb mounted inside a metal canister (to cut out the light, which may harm the developing embryos) that may be attached to the inside back of the box. A thermostat placed near the area where the eggs are kept should be set to maintain the temperature inside the incubator at about 30°C (86°F). With such an incubator it is not really necessary to use an incubation medium. The eggs can be placed on an acrylic sheet into which depressions have been drilled for each individual egg. A tray of water is placed in the base of the incubator and the acrylic sheet is mounted about 15 cm above this. To increase humidity, the water may be heated with a thermostatically controlled aquarium heater. Care should be taken to top up the water at regular intervals. The high humidity and the excellent circulation of air around the eggs make this a highly successful method.

At hatching time, the young

Above: *There is a strong tendency for most or all the eggs in a nest to hatch at about the same time or at least for the babies to emerge at about the same time and then disperse. This is especially true in turtles that nest in sand along large bodies of water, either the sea or large lakes and rivers. These hatchling* Podocnemis unifilis *will soon disappear into the bottom of the lake.*

chelonian will first make a small hole in the egg shell with its egg tooth (which will be absorbed soon after hatching) and will eventually break the shell wide open before crawling free. Ensure that there are no spaces between the walls of the incubator and the acrylic sheet through which the young reptiles can fall into the water and drown. The time taken to hatch varies from individual to individual, some emerging in a few minutes, others taking several hours. The yolk sac will still be attached to the center of the plastron and will take a few hours to be absorbed. No attempt should be made to remove this sac or to interfere with the hatching process, except on the rare occasions that complications set in. Occasionally a slow hatcher may become attached to the shell due to the egg fluid drying out too rapidly. In such cases the hatchling may be placed in a shallow dish of lukewarm water and gently swabbed until it is free.

Rearing

Probably the most difficult part of turtle breeding is the rearing of the young. As soon as the hatchlings have absorbed their yolk sacs and are moving freely about they should be removed to a nursery cage that is maintained at about 27°C (81°F). They should be provided with a shallow dish kept topped up with fresh water and fed only sparingly for the first few days. Quite often they will refuse all food for about a week after hatching but should be provided with small, tender bits of foods similar to those suggested for the adults. Soon they will start feeding regularly.

One problem that frequently arises in the rearing of chelonians is that the shell may grow erratically due to overfeeding with high-protein foods coupled with a lack of calcium and phosphorus in the diet. It is therefore important to feed sparingly, but also to ensure that adequate mineral and vitamin supplements are included.

It is not recommended that turtles be hibernated in their first year; nor should they be kept outside except on very warm days, when they will benefit from the natural sunlight.

Below: The joys of "turtlehood."

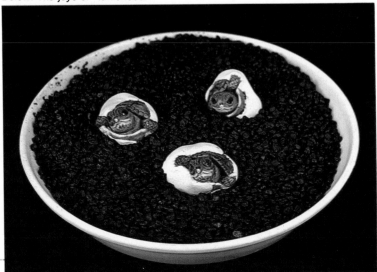

Bibliography

Breen, John F. 1974. *Encyclopedia of Reptiles and Amphibians.* T.F.H. Publications, Neptune, NJ.

Conant, Roger. 1975. *A Field Guide to Reptiles and Amphibians of Eastern and Central North America.* Houghton Mifflin, Boston, MA.

Ernst, Carl H. and Roger W. Barbour. 1972. *Turtles of the United States.* Univ. Kentucky Press, Lexington, KY.

Freiberg, Marcos. 1981. *Turtles of South America.* T.F.H. Publications, Neptune, NJ.

Jocher, Willy, 1973. *Turtles for Home and Garden.* T.F.H. Publications, Neptune, NJ.

Masters, Charles O. 1975. *Encyclopedia of Live Foods.* T.F.H. Publications, Neptune, NJ.

Mehrtens, John M. 1984. *Turtles.* T.F.H. Publications, Neptune, NJ.

Pope, Clifford H. 1955. *The Reptile World.* A. A. Knopf, New York.

Pritchard, Peter C. H. 1979. *Encyclopedia of Turtles.* T.F.H. Publications, Neptune, NJ. (Absolutely essential reading for the advanced hobbyist.)

Pritchard, Peter C. H. and Pedro Trebbau. 1984. *The Turtles of Venezuela.* Soc. Study Amph. and Rept., Oxford, Ohio.

Smith, Hobart M. and Edmund D. Brodie, Jr. 1982. *A Guide to Field Identification: Reptiles of North America.* Golden Press, New York.

Zimmerman, Elke. 1986. *Breeding Terrarium Animals.* T.F.H. Publications, Neptune, NJ.

Right: *With proper care, many of the hardy species of turtles and tortoises will make good pets, but they cannot be neglected.*

Picture Credits

Pelham Aldrich-Blake, 35 Top
American Museum of Natural History, 74
Dr. Herbert R. Axelrod, 5, 29, 37, 44, 48, 53, 54 Top, 57, 59, 61, 65 Top, 70, 78, 80, 82, 99, 103, 106, 119, 121
Patrick Burchfield, 55
Tom Caravaglia, 56, 69, 75 Bottom
Herb Davis, 109
Helmut Debelius, 13
Dr. Guido Dingerkus, 14
Keith Gillett, *Aust. Great Barrier Reef,* 20, 90
Michael Gilroy, 52
Bob Gossington, 114
Rogelio Gutierrez, 97
John M. Mehrtens, 73, 75 Top
Horst Mueller, 7
Klaus Peter, 98
Dr. Peter C. H. Pritchard, 11, 17, 22, 23, 26, 30, 31, 32, 33, 35 Bottom, 36, 38, 39, 40, 41, 42, 58, 62, 63, 64, 66, 68, 72, 76, 83, 84, 88, 89, 93, 101, 111, 128
Harald Schultz, 2, 77, 92, 118, 123
Courtsey Dr. D. Terver, Nancy Aquarium, France, 51 (Cl. Poivre), 79 (V. Bels), 94 (Cl. Poivre)
John Visser, 65 Bottom
K. and D. Zinck, 18, 45, 47

Right: *The ultimate fate of too many turtles is still to be collected and eaten, as shown here for market groups of* Geochelone denticulata *and* Podocnemis expansa *in Brazil. Unfortunately, many native economies depend on turtles and their eggs for protein, and without this source of food they could not survive. For many turtles their only hope for the future is to be bred in captivity.*

Index

The emydid turtle species Batagur baska. *Drawing by Peter Parks.*